BAZI STRUCTURES

&

Structural Useful Gods

FIRE 火

丙 Bing
丁 Ding

格局與格局用神

BaZi Structures & Structural Useful Gods
Fire Structure

The author can be reached at:

Mastery Academy of Chinese Metaphysics Sdn. Bhd. (611143-A)
19-3, The Boulevard, Mid Valley City,
59200 Kuala Lumpur, Malaysia.
Tel   : +603-2284 8080
Fax   : +603-2284 1218
Email   : info@masteryacademy.com
Website: www.masteryacademy.com

DISCLAIMER:

Published by JY Books Sdn. Bhd. (659134-T)

Table of Contents

Bing 丙 Fire Day Master, Born in :

Table of Contents

About The Chinese Metaphysics Reference Series

Reference Series

The Chinese Metaphysics Reference Series of books are designed primarily to be used as complimentary textbooks for scholars, students, researchers, teachers and practitioners of Chinese Metaphysics.

The goal is to provide quick easy reference tables, diagrams and charts, facilitating the study and practice of various Chinese Metaphysics subjects including Feng Shui, BaZi, Yi Jing, Zi Wei, Liu Ren, Ze Ri, Ta Yi, Qi Men and Mian Xiang.

This series of books are intended as reference text and educational materials principally for the academic syllabuses of the **Mastery Academy of Chinese Metaphysics**. The contents have also been formatted so that Feng Shui Masters and other teachers of Chinese Metaphysics will always have a definitive source of reference at hand, when teaching or applying their art.

Because each school of Chinese Metaphysics is different, the Reference Series of books usually do not contain any specific commentaries, application methods or explanations on the theory behind the formulas presented in its contents. This is to ensure that the contents can be used freely and independently by all Feng Shui Masters and teachers of Chinese Metaphysics without conflict.

If you would like to study or learn the applications of any of the formulas presented in the Reference Series of books, we recommend that you undertake the courses offered by Joey Yap and his team of Instructors at the Mastery Academy of Chinese Metaphysics.

Titles offers in the Reference Series:

1. The Chinese Metaphysics Compendium
2. Dong Gong Date Selection
3. Earth Study Discern Truth
4. Xuan Kong Da Gua Structure Reference Book
5. San Yuan Dragon Gate Eight Formations Water Method
6. Xuan Kong Da Gua Ten Thousand Year Calendar
7. Plum Blossom Divination Reference Book
8. The Date Selection Compendium (Book 1) - The 60 Jia Zi Attributes
9. BaZi Structures & Structural Useful Gods Reference Series

Preface

The study and practice of BaZi is an infinitely rewarding and intriguing one, with literally an inexhaustible depth and range from which we can mine our information on a person's character, temperament, life outlook and personal destiny. The simplest data – your birth date and time – can yield a rich treasure trove of knowledge, most of which can help shed new light on old perceptions.

The idea for this BaZi Structures and Structural Useful God Reference Series came out of a common need among my BaZi students, many of whom wanted to learn more about how the various structures in BaZi are derived. This series was therefore created to help students learn and absorb the methods and techniques in which a structure is created and developed mainly from a classical standpoint.

While initially it was my idea to create one BaZi Structures book to accommodate all 10 Heavenly Stems (Day Masters), I soon found out that it would not be a book that could reasonably be used by anyone – because it would be too heavy to lift! So I decided to break it apart into five different books, with each one corresponding to each Element. The book you're holding in your hands is on Fire Structures, for both Bing 丙 and Ding 丁 Ding Day Masters.

There are many traditional sources available on the BaZi structures, and the derivation of those structures. One of the more well-known texts is the *Qiong Tong Bao Jian* 窮通寶鑑, written by a famous master, *Xu Le Wu* 徐樂吾. Another popular BaZi scholar of recent past who contributed a lot to mainstream BaZi theories, especially those relating to structures, is *Wei Qian Li* 韋千里.

It's difficult for most students to have access to this information because it's scattered about in various texts and documents, and also – all of it is available only in Chinese. It was my intention, therefore, to compile this information into one convenient source, and to present the transliterated version of these traditional texts for the modern, English-speaking practitioner and student without losing the essence of the original.

To derive a structure and structural Useful God in BaZi, one must know and understand the Day Master and the month of birth, and its variations in a BaZi chart. There are traditional methods on how this is derived, and there are newer interpretations on these methods.

As such, different practitioners and teachers have different methods and formats to derive these structures, and it is recommended that you use the techniques outlined in this book with care and thought. As always, there is much merit in

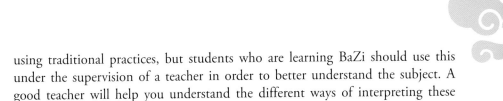

using traditional practices, but students who are learning BaZi should use this under the supervision of a teacher in order to better understand the subject. A good teacher will help you understand the different ways of interpreting these traditional texts.

Do note that these texts should not be taken literally. Different masters may agree or disagree with the classical commentaries included here, and as a student, it's important for you to know the reasons why. Better yet, it's important for you to know those reasons and then go on to form your own conclusions, based on your understanding of the various interpretations.

For that reason, this book was designed to be a reference accompaniment for the students of my BaZi Mastery Series, where you'll be able to get the guidance you need in interpreting these traditional methods. I encourage you to take a class because it will help to place this material in context and give you the added knowledge you need to help you make the most of the information contained within this book. Each and every structure in this book could be its own chapter, because it can literally explain a person and his or her modus operandi!

I hope you enjoy your research on this subject, and here's to many pleasurable hours of BaZi Structural study!

Warm regards,

Joey Yap
July 2009

Author's personal websites :
www.joeyyap.com I www.fengshuilogy.com (Personal blog)

Academy websites :
www.masteryacademy.com I www.masteryjournal.com I www.maelearning.com

Follow Joey's current updates on Twitter :
www.twitter.com/joeyyap

MASTERY ACADEMY
OF CHINESE METAPHYSICS™

At **www.masteryacademy.com**, you will find some useful tools to ascertain key information about the Feng Shui of a property or for the study of Astrology.

The Joey Yap Flying Stars Calculator can be utilised to plot your home or office Flying Stars chart. To find out your personal best directions, use the 8 Mansions Calculator. To learn more about your personal Destiny, you can use the Joey Yap BaZi Ming Pan Calculator to plot your Four Pillars of Destiny – you just need to have your date of birth (day, month, year) and time of birth.

For more information about BaZi, Xuan Kong or Flying Star Feng Shui, or if you wish to learn more about these subjects with Joey Yap, logon to the Mastery Academy of Chinese Metaphysics website at **www.masteryacademy.com.**

MASTERY ACADEMY
E-LEARNING CENTER
www.maelearning.com

www.maelearning.com

Bookmark this address on your computer, and visit this newly-launched website today. With the E-Learning Center, knowledge of Chinese Metaphysics is a mere 'click' away!

Our E-Learning Center consists of 3 distinct components.

1. Online Courses
These shall comprise of 3 Programs: our Online Feng Shui Program, Online BaZi Program, and Online Mian Xiang Program. Each lesson contains a video lecture, slide presentation and downloadable course notes.

2. MA Live!
With MA Live!, Joey Yap's workshops, tutorials, courses and seminars on various Chinese Metaphysics subjects broadcasted right to your computer screen. Better still, participants will not only get to see and hear Joey talk 'live', but also get to engage themselves directly in the event and more importantly, TALK to Joey via the MA Live! interface. All the benefits of a live class, minus the hassle of actually having to attend one!

3. Video-On-Demand (VOD)
Get immediate streaming-downloads of the Mastery Academy's wide range of educational DVDs, right on your computer screen. No more shipping costs and waiting time to be incurred!

Study at your own pace, and interact with your Instructor and fellow students worldwide… at your own convenience and privacy. With our E-Learning Center, knowledge of Chinese Metaphysics is brought DIRECTLY to you in all its clarity, with illustrated presentations and comprehensive notes expediting your learning curve!

Welcome to the Mastery Academy's E-LEARNING CENTER…YOUR virtual gateway to Chinese Metaphysics mastery!

Introduction - Fire Day Masters

Fire Day Masters are usually warm, friendly, expressive, passionate and even compassionate. Nevertheless, since there is a significant deal of difference between Bing 丙 Fire and Ding 丁 Fire Day Masters, it would be best to analyze them separately.

A Bing Fire Day Master – like the sun – radiates warmth, and can be very vibrant and vivacious in appearance. They also tend to be sincere, just and noble, without a hidden agenda.

While they may be proud and even egoistic, they are not the type to harbor grudges and will passionately fight or champion a cause they believe to be worthy. Bing Fire Day Masters are often routine-oriented, although this means they can eventually become bored with their jobs or work!

Meanwhile, Ding Fire Day Masters, being Yin in polarity, tend to be natural leaders and great motivators. They can also rise to the occasion when needed, and are meticulous, detail-oriented and sentimental by nature.

Do not be surprised, however, if a Ding Fire Day Master becomes de-motivated by him or herself – simply because this person was too busy igniting the proverbial fire in others, whilst forgetting to light his/her own fire!

Bing (丙) Fire Day Master

Overview:

Bing 丙 Fire is Yang Fire, and hence represents strong, blazing quantities of Fire, such as the sun.

A Bing Fire Day Master – like the sun – radiates warmth, and can be very vibrant and vivacious in appearance. They also tend to be sincere, just and noble, without a hidden agenda.

Bing Fire Day Masters are, however, the show-offish type; usually displaying a strong – even overwhelming – desire to triumph and succeed, no matter the odds. Those born in a month where Wood and Fire happen to be strong will, however, find their chances of success more greatly enhanced.

Although they may be proud and even egoistic, Bing Fire people are not the type to harbor grudges and will passionately fight or champion a cause they believe to be worthy. And just like the sun, they are often routine-oriented - although this means they can eventually become bored with their jobs or work!

Where Metal and Water are present in strength and weaken a Bing Fire Day Master, significant changes may lurk just around the corner, for this Day Master.

Bing 丙 Fire Day Master, Born in First Month 正月

Yin 寅 (Tiger) Month
February 4th – March 5th

Do note that the dates provided above are subject to slight yearly variations. Please refer to the Ten Thousand Year Calendar for the accurate transition dates for each year.

| Day Master | Bing 丙 Fire | Month | Yin 寅 (Tiger) |

Tiger

日元 Day Master	月 Month
丙 *Bing* **Yang Fire**	寅 *Yin* **Tiger** **Yang Wood**

For a Bing Fire Day Master born in a Yin (Tiger) Month, an Indirect Resource Structure is formed where Jia Wood is revealed as one of the Heavenly Stems.

Where Wu Earth is revealed as one of the Heavenly Stems, an Eating God Structure is formed.

Where Bing Fire is revealed as one of the Heavenly Stems, Thriving Structure may be formed depending on the condition of the chart.

Should, however, neither Jia Wood , Bing Fire nor Wu Earth happen to be revealed within the Heavenly Stems, one should select the BaZi Chart's most prominent Qi attribute at one's discretion.

| Day Master | Bing 丙 Fire | Month | Yin 寅 (Tiger) |

喜用神提要 Regulating Useful God Reference Guide

月 Month	用神 Useful God	
1st Month 正月 Yin 寅 (Tiger) Month	**壬** *Ren* **Yang Water**	**庚** *Geng* **Yang Metal**

For a Yin (Tiger) Month, Ren Water and Geng Metal are its Regulating Useful Gods.

Ren Water is the primary Useful God to this Day Master. Meanwhile, Geng Metal serves as a supporting Useful God to produce and ensure the continuity of Ren Water.

正月
First Month

Tiger

5

正
月

First Month

| **Day Master** | Bing 丙 Fire | **Month** | Yin 寅 (Tiger) |

4th day of February – 5th day of March, Gregorian Calendar

Where both Wood and Fire are present, they would produce and strengthen this Bing Fire Day Master.

Insofar as Useful Gods are concerned, Ren Water is noted for its ability to transform and reflect the attributes of this Bing Fire Day Master. Meanwhile, Metal is also simultaneously needed to produce Water.

Where Earth is present in abundance, this Day Master shall belong to an intelligent and wealthy person. One who's exceptionally talented.

Tiger

Day Master	Bing 丙 Fire	Month	Yin 寅 (Tiger)

Commentary

In addition to the preceding narratives on the potential Structures and scenarios resulting from a Bing Fire Day Master born in a Yin (Tiger) Month, the following circumstances also play their respective roles in determining the overall strength of this Day Master's BaZi Chart.

Note:

- Ren Water is the primary Useful God for this Day Master.

- It is undesirable for Ji Earth to penetrate to the Heavenly Stems of the chart.

- Bing Fire is not very strong in a Yin (Tiger) Month, as the timing of the year also represents the transition between winter and spring. Bing Fire at this time depicts the sunlight that begins to exert its warmth, with the passing of the cold, dark winter months.

- The role of Ren Water here is not to control Bing Fire. Instead, its presence allows Bing Fire – which is akin to sunlight – to shine and simmer on the surface of water, therefore painting a sentimental 'picture' of this Day Master.

- Bing Fire should never be separated from Ren Water; just as Ren Water should not be separated from Geng Metal. This is why Ren Water is the primary Useful God to this Day Master, with Geng Metal serving as its secondary Useful God.

- Where Ji Earth is present as inside the Branches, this Day Master would belong to a skillful, knowledgeable person– and this star would enable him or her to achieve a high level of success, authority and status in life.

- Where Ji Earth and Ren Water are revealed in the Heavenly Stems – this Day Master would probably possess a bold, even foolhardy personality, and perhaps even be inclined towards committing mischief in life. It is only in the presence of Wu Earth that the preceding situation may be negated and its outcomes duly averted.

- Where Geng Metal (the Indirect Wealth Star) and Xin Metal (the Direct Wealth Star) are both penetrated to the Heavenly Stems, this Day Master would only be able to lead an average life, at best.

- Where the Indirect Resource Star is seen or revealed in the Heavenly Stems, this Day Master would be a learned, knowledgeable one.

正
月

First Month

Tiger

| Day Master | Bing 丙 Fire | Month | Yin 寅 (Tiger) |

Commentary

- Where two Direct Wealth Stars (Xin Metal) are revealed in the Heavenly Stems – compete with one another to combine with Bing Fire to form Water – under such circumstances – regardless of whether it is a male or female chart – this person may be plagued by alcoholism in life, as well as possess a lascivious, even lewd, personality. He or she will also lack a sense of direction and purpose in life, and find it hard to succeed in whatever endeavors he or she may undertake.

- Where Geng Metal and Xin Metal are not present at all, this person would be inclined towards leading only a very simple and humble life.

- Where Wu Earth penetrates to the Heavenly Stems – and while Jia Wood is not simultaneously revealed – this person may find it difficult to establish him or herself, career-wise, and as a result, may be afflicted by poverty in life.

- Where the Earthly Branches form a Fire Structure, Wu Earth must not penetrate to the Heavenly Stems of the chart. Otherwise, this Day Master may only be able to lead an average or even mediocre life, at best. This holds true, even if Ren Water is also present in the Heavenly Stems.

- Even if the Earthly Branches form a Fire Structure, Fire is nonetheless still relatively weak in a Yin (Tiger) Month. As such, this Day Master may still be afflicted by loneliness in life.

- Where Gui Water is used in the absence of Ren Water, all structures are only sub-standard.

| Day Master | Bing 丙 Fire | Month | Yin 寅 (Tiger) |

Additional Attributes

Tiger

格局 Structural Star	七殺 Seven Killings	偏財 Indirect Wealth
用神 Useful God	Ren 壬 Water	Geng 庚 Metal
Conditions	\multicolumn{2}{l}{Where both Ren Water and Geng Metal are revealed, this Day Master shall enjoy great success in his or her career-related pursuits. Where only Ren Water is revealed – but Geng Metal is not – this Day Master would still possess a generous, charismatic and magnanimous personality.}
Positive Circumstances	\multicolumn{2}{l}{Ren Water and Geng Metal appearing in the Heavenly Stems.}
Negative Circumstances	\multicolumn{2}{l}{The Geng Metal is found atop a Shen (Monkey) Earthly Branch to form a Geng Shen Pillar. In addition, the Shen (Monkey) Earthly Branch clashes with the Yin (Tiger) Earthly Branch.}

格局 Structural Star	七殺 Seven Killings	正官 Direct Officer
用神 Useful God	Ren 壬 Water	Gui 癸 Water
Conditions	\multicolumn{2}{l}{Where the Earthly Branches form a full Water Structure, Wu Earth must also be present to keep Water under control. It would also be preferable to have Bing Fire (a Friend Star) and Ding Fire (a Rob Wealth Star) present.}
Positive Circumstances	\multicolumn{2}{l}{In the absence of Ren Water, Gui Water may be used in its stead. Nevertheless, Gui Water must be rooted in the Earth Branches. Otherwise, this Day Master may be particularly susceptible to eye-related ailments in life.}
Negative Circumstances	\multicolumn{2}{l}{Where Ren Water (Seven Killings Star) is present in abundance – but there is no Wu Earth (Eating God Star) to control it – this Day Master may possess a foolhardy personality, and also possibly prone towards committing mischief in life.}

| Day Master | Bing 丙 Fire | Month | Yin 寅 (Tiger) |

Additional Attributes

格局 Structural Star	偏財 Indirect Wealth
用神 Useful God	Geng 庚 Metal
Conditions	Where Geng Metal (Indirect Wealth Star) is revealed in the Hour or Month Pillars' Heavenly Stems, this person would be a learned, cultivated and knowledgeable .
Positive Circumstances	Absense of Xin Metal
Negative Circumstances	Geng Metal intermingles with Xin Metal (Direct Wealth Star).

格局 Structural Star	正財 Direct Wealth
用神 Useful God	Xin 辛 Metal
Conditions	Where Xin Metal is the Heavenly Stem of the Year and Hour Pillars, a 'greedy' combination takes place, since both Xin Metal elements will compete with one another to combine with Bing Fire. Under such circumstances, this Day Master may be prone towards alcoholism, as well as lewd or lascivious behaviour in life. He or she may even squander away any inheritance passed down from his or her elders or ancestors.
Positive Circumstances	A distance between the Day Master and the Xin Metal.
Negative Circumstances	Xin Metal in the Month and Hour Stems.

| Day Master | Bing 丙 Fire | | Month | Yin 寅 (Tiger) |

Additional Attributes

格局 Structural Star	食神 Eating God
用神 Useful God	Wu 戊 Earth
Conditions	Where Wu Earth (Eating God Star) is found in abundance, Jia Wood should also penetrate to the Heavenly Stems. Otherwise, this Day Master may be afflicted by poverty throughout his or her entire life.
Positive Circumstances	Jia Wood (Indirect Resource) Star penetrates to the Heavenly Stems.
Negative Circumstances	Jia Wood and Wu Earth side by side on the Stems.

Tiger

格局 Structural Star	比肩 Friend	劫財 Rob Wealth
用神 Useful God	Bing 丙 Fire	Ding 丁 Fire
Conditions	Where a Fire Structure is formed in the Branches, Gui Water must not be present.	
Positive Circumstances	Presence of Ren Water.	
Negative Circumstances	Gui Water in the form of Zi is found in the chart.	

* *Ren Water and Geng Metal are preferred Useful Gods for a Bing Fire Day Master born in a Yin (Tiger) Month.*

BaZi Structures & Structural Useful Gods 格局與格局用神

| Day Master | Bing 丙 Fire | Month | Yin 寅 (Tiger) |

Summary

- It would not be favorable, where Ding Fire (Rob Wealth Star) is revealed. This is because Ding Fire combines with Ren Water to form Wood. And under such circumstances, this Day Master would only stand to lose Ren Water – which is an important Regulating Useful God.

Tiger

Bing 丙 Fire Day Master, Born in Second Month 二月

Mao 卯 (Rabbit) Month
March 6th – April 4th

Do note that the dates provided above are subject to slight yearly variations. Please refer to the Ten Thousand Year Calendar for the accurate transition dates for each year.

Day Master Bing 丙 Fire   **Month** Mao 卯 (Rabbit)

Rabbit

日元 **Day Master**	月 **Month**
丙 *Bing* **Yang Fire**	卯 *Mao* **Rabbit** **Yin Wood**

For a Bing Fire Day Master born in a Mao (Rabbit) Month, a Direct Resource Structure is formed where Yi Wood is revealed as one of the Heavenly Stems.

Even if Yi Wood is not revealed as a Heavenly Stem, a Direct Resource Structure would still be considered to have been formed.

Day Master	Bing 丙 Fire	Month	Mao 卯 (Rabbit)

喜用神提要 Regulating Useful God Reference Guide

月 Month	用神 Useful God
2nd Month 二月 Mao 卯 (Rabbit) Month	壬 Ren **Yang Water** 己 Ji **Yin Earth**

For a Mao (Rabbit) Month, Ren Water and Ji Earth are its Regulating Useful Gods.

Priority should be given to Ren Water as this Day Master's primary Useful God. Where Ren Water is present in abundance, Wu Earth may be used to keep it under control.

Where Bing Fire is weak, Wood – this Day Master's Resource Stars – may be used for support.

In the absence of Ren Water, Ji Earth may be used as yet another Useful God in its stead.

二月 Second Month

Rabbit

15

| Day Master | Bing 丙 Fire | Month | Mao 卯 (Rabbit) |

6th day of March – 4th day of April, Gregorian Calendar

Bing Fire is considered strong in this month due to the presence of vibrant Wood.

Since Wood and Fire is strong, it is inferred that Metal and Water are this Day Master's important Useful Gods.

Metal is needed to keep Wood under control - as well as to produce Water.

Where this criteria is met, Female Day Masters, with strong Self Elements, should be able to attract and marry fairly prosperous or affluent husbands in life. In addition, they will also be blessed with a high level of status and authority in life, due to the influence and support of their husbands.

二月 Second Month

卯 Rabbit

Day Master	Bing 丙 Fire		Month	Mao 卯 (Rabbit)

Commentary

In addition to the preceding narratives on the potential Structures and scenarios resulting from a Bing Fire Day Master born in a Mao (Rabbit) Month, the following circumstances also play their respective roles in determining the overall strength of this Day Master's BaZi Chart.

Note:

- Ren Water is the primary Useful God to this Day Master.

- It is undesirable to have Ding Fire revealed in the Heavenly Stems, since it combines with Ren Water to form Wood.

- Where Ji Earth is seen intermingling with and possibly 'contaminating' Ren Water, this Day Master may only be able to lead an average life, at best.

- Although Ren Water is the primary Useful God to this Day Master, Geng Metal – as a secondary Useful God - should not be missing or absent from the chart.

- Where Ren Water is not seen or revealed in the Heavenly Stems, Ji Earth may be used to replace it as a Useful God. Nevertheless, under such circumstances, this Day Master may only be able to lead a slightly above average or mediocre life, at best.

- Where Ren Water is presence in abundance in the Heavenly Stems, Wu Earth may be used to keep it under control. In any case, Ji Earth should not be seen intermingling with - and hence 'contaminating' - Ren Water.

- Where Ren Water is present in all four pillars – while Wu Earth is absent from the Heavenly Stems – this Day Master may be inclined towards leading a wandering, possibly even aimless, life.

- A Day Master also born in a Xin Metal in the Hour or Month Stem may establish and carve a niche for him or herself, as far as career-related pursuits are concerned. However, there is a negative set back as the Xin Metal and Bing Fire seeks to combine. It is only with the presence of Ding Fire element that the preceding scenario may be duly averted. Without Ding Fire to counter and control Xin Metal, this Day Master may be prone towards alcoholism, lewd or lascivious behavior and squandering any inheritance he or she receives in life.

- Where Ren Water is available and employed as a Useful God to this Day Master, Jia Wood should be present in the chart, in order to prevent Wu Earth from exerting an overly strong control over Ren Water.

- It would not be preferable to have more than two Direct Wealth Stars (Xin Metal) present, since both will invariably compete with each other to combine with Bing Fire to form Water.

二月 Second Month

Rabbit

BaZi Structures & Structural Useful Gods 格局與格局用神

Day Master Bing 丙 Fire		Month Mao 卯 (Rabbit)

Additional Attributes

格局 Structural Star	七殺 Seven Killings	偏財 Indirect Wealth	正財 Direct Wealth
用神 Useful God	Ren 壬 Water	Geng 庚 Metal	Xin 辛 Metal

Conditions	Where Ren Water and Geng Metal are all present, this Day Master shall prosper in life. In the absence of Ren Water and Gui Water, Ji Earth may be 'borrowed' as a substitute Useful God. Nevertheless, under such circumstances, this Day Master may find it hard to truly succeed or prosper in life; no matter how skillful or talented he or she may be.
Positive Circumstances	Where Wu Earth is revealed and exerts a strong control over Ren Water, Jia Wood is needed to counter and keep Wu Earth under control.
Negative Circumstances	Ding Fire (Rob Wealth Star) combines with Ren Water (Seven Killings Star) to form Wood. Or presence of Wu Earth which exerts an overly strong control over Ren Water

Day Master	Bing 丙 Fire		Month	Mao 卯 (Rabbit)

Additional Attributes

格局 Structural Star	七殺 Seven Killings	正官 Direct Officer
用神 Useful God	Ren 壬 Water	Gui 癸 Water
Conditions	Where the Earthly Branches form a Direct Officer or Seven Killings Structure with this Day Master, Wu Earth (Eating God Star) is needed to keep Water under control.	
Positive Circumstances	Wu Earth (Eating God Star) is revealed in the Heavenly Stems.	
Negative Circumstances	Without Wu Earth, this Day Master may be prone towards leading a wandering, possibly even aimless life. Where Metal is present in abundance and produces Water, any structure formed would still be a substandard one.	

Rabbit

格局 Structural Star	食神 Eating God
用神 Useful God	Wu 戊 Earth
Conditions	Where Wu Earth (Eating God Star) is present in abundance, Ren Water (Seven Killings Star) is still needed as a Useful God to this Day Master.
Positive Circumstances	Presence of Jia Wood.
Negative Circumstances	Earth Luck Pillars are undesirable.

* *Geng Metal and Ren Water are the preferred Useful Gods for a Bing Fire Day Master born in a Mao (Rabbit) Month.*

BaZi Structures & Structural Useful Gods 格局與格局用神

Day Master	Bing 丙 Fire	Month	Mao 卯 (Rabbit)

Summary

- Ding Fire element is only needed to counter and weaken Xin Metal when it is present.

Rabbit

Bing 丙 Fire Day Master, Born in Third Month 三月

Chen 辰 (Dragon) Month
April 5th - May 5th

Do note that the dates provided above are subject to slight yearly variations. Please refer to the Ten Thousand Year Calendar for the accurate transition dates for each year.

| Day Master | Bing 丙 Fire | Month | Chen 辰 (Dragon) |

日元 Day Master	月 Month
丙 *Bing* **Yang Fire**	辰 *Chen* **Dragon** **Yang Earth**

For a Bing Fire Day Master born in a Chen (Dragon) Month, an Eating God Structure is formed where Wu Earth is revealed as one of the Heavenly Stems.

Where Yi Wood is revealed as one of the Heavenly Stems, a Direct Resource Structure is formed.

Where Gui Water is revealed as one of the Heavenly Stems, a Direct Officer Structure is formed.

Should, however, neither Wu Earth nor Yi Wood nor Gui Water happen to be revealed within the Heavenly Stems, one should select a Structure according to the BaZi Chart's most prominent Qi attribute at one's discretion.

| Day Master | Bing 丙 Fire | Month | Chen 辰 (Dragon) |

喜用神提要 **Regulating Useful God Reference Guide**

月 Month	用神 Useful God	
3rd Month 三月 Chen 辰 (Dragon) Month	壬 *Ren* **Yang Water**	甲 *Jia* **Yang Wood**

三月 Third Month

Dragon

For a Chen (Dragon) Month, Ren Water and Jia Wood are its most important Regulating Useful Gods.

Priority should always be accorded Ren Water – as this Day Master's primary Useful God.

Meanwhile, where Earth is present in abundance, Jia Wood may be employed as a secondary Useful God to keep Earth under control.

BaZi Structures & Structural Useful Gods 格局與格局用神

Day Master Bing 丙 Fire	Month Chen 辰 (Dragon)

5th day of April – 5th day of May, Gregorian Calendar

三
月

Third Month

Earth is prominent in a Chen (Dragon) Month. It would exert a strong influence over Ren Water.

This is why Water – in strength and abundance – is required as a primary Useful God to overcome the preceding scenario. And where Earth is strong, Wood may also be used to 'loosen', weaken and hence keep it under control.

Meanwhile, Metal is the selected as Useful God when Fire Qi is in abundance.

Dragon

Day Master	Bing 丙 Fire	Month	Chen 辰 (Dragon)

Commentary

In addition to the preceding narratives on the potential Structures and scenarios resulting from a Bing Fire Day Master born in a Chen (Dragon) Month, the following circumstances also play their respective roles in determining the overall strength of this Day Master's BaZi Chart.

Dragon

Note:

- Priority should be accorded Ren Water as the primary Useful God. Jia Wood, as the secondary Regulating Useful God.

- Whenever Earth is in abundance, Jia Wood is needed.

- It is however, undesirable to have Ji Earth penetrating to the Heavenly Stems.

- Where Ren Water and Jia Wood are both revealed, this Day Master shall enjoy great success in his or her career and a life of status and recognition. However, it is undesirable to have Geng Metal penetrate to the Heavenly Stems in this case. This is because Wood is split by Metal. When this is the case, this person may only enjoy a mediocre life at best.

- Where Ren Water is revealed in the Heavenly Stems – but Jia Wood remains hidden amongst the Earthly Branches – this person can still prosper and become wealthy in life; although his or her authority is not the same status as his / her wealth.

- Where Jia Wood is revealed in the Heavenly Stems – but Ren Water is missing from chart – this Day Master may be afflicted by loneliness and mediocrity in life.

- Where neither Ren Water nor Jia Wood is found in the Heavenly Stems – but Ren Water can be found as one of the Earthly Branches' Hidden Stems, although Jia Wood remains totally missing from chart – this person may only lead a simple, humble life at best; no matter how knowledgeable or learned he or she may be.

- Where Ren Water and Jia Wood are completely absent from the chart, this Day Master will probably lead a life that is a lackluster.

- Where Ren Water and Jia Wood are both revealed in the Heavenly Stems, Geng Metal must not penetrate to the Heavenly Stems, at the same time. Without Ren Water and Jia Wood in the Heavenly Stems, however, Geng Metal must penetrate to the Heavenly Stems.

- Where Ding Fire and Ji Earth are both seen in the Heavenly Stems, this Day Master may not be able to achieve high levels of success despite how learned and skillful he/she is.

- Where the Shen (Monkey), Zi (Rat) and Chen (Dragon) Earthly Branches form a Water Structure, it would be unsuitable for Ren Water to be revealed and penetrate to the Heavenly Stems.

- Where Water structure is formed and Ren Water also revealed, Wu Earth must penetrate to the Heavenly Stems.

- Where Wu Earth does not penetrate to the Heavenly Stems but instead remains as one of the Earthly Branches' Hidden Stems, this Day Master would also suffer mediocrity. Life would be filled with setbacks and hassles.

- Where the Yin (Tiger), Wu (Horse) and Xu (Dog) Earthly Branches form a Fire Structure – while Bing Fire or Ding Fire is also seen in the Heavenly Stems – Wu Earth must penetrate to the Heavenly Stems. Wu Earth governs the stability of the chart.

| Day Master | Bing 丙 Fire | Month | Chen 辰 (Dragon) |

Additional Attributes

三月 Third Month

辰 Dragon

格局 Structural Star	七殺 Seven Killings	偏印 Indirect Resource
用神 Useful God	Ren 壬 Water	Jia 甲 Wood
Conditions	Where Ren Water and Jia Wood are present as Useful Gods, this Day Master shall enjoy great success in career and in life.	
Positive Circumstances	Where Jia Wood remains hidden, Geng Metal must penetrate to the Heavenly Stems.	
Negative Circumstances	Where Geng Metal and Xin Metal are revealed and attack the Jia Wood, this Day Master may not really succeed or prosper in life; no matter how knowledgeable or intelligent he or she may be.	

26

Day Master	Bing 丙 Fire		Month	Chen 辰 (Dragon)

三月 Third Month

Additional Attributes

格局 Structural Star	食神 Eating God	傷官 Hurting Officer
用神 Useful God	Wu 戊 Earth	Ji 己 Earth
Conditions	Where the Earthly Branches form an Earth Structure, Jia Wood is needed.	
Positive Circumstances	Jia Wood penetrated to the Heavenly Stems.	
Negative Circumstances	Absense of Jia Wood.	

Dragon

* Ren Water is the primary Useful God for a Bing Fire Day Master born in a Chen (Dragon) Month.

** Where the Earthly Branches form an Earth Structure, Jia Wood is needed as a Useful God to keep Earth under control; although Ren Water must not be absent or missing as well.

27

三月 Third Month

Dragon

| Day Master | Bing 丙 Fire | Month | Chen 辰 (Dragon) |

Summary

- Ren Water (Seven Killings Star) and Jia Wood (Indirect Resource Star) play important roles as Useful Gods to this Day Master.

- Where Ren Water (Seven Killings Star) is revealed – but Jia Wood (Indirect Resource Star) remains hidden – this Day Master may prosper in life; although he or she may not enjoy a corresponding level of status or authority with his or her wealth.

- Where Ren Water is not revealed in the Heavenly Stems, with Jia Wood is totally absent, this Day Master may only be able to lead an average life at best; regardless of how knowledgeable and intelligent he or she may be.

- Where both Ren Water and Jia Wood are completely missing, this Day Master may find it difficult to succeed or progress in life; regardless of which Luck Period he or she enters.

Bing 丙 Fire Day Master, Born in Fourth Month 四月

Si 巳 (Snake) Month
May 6th - June 5th

Do note that the dates provided above are subject to slight yearly variations. Please refer to the Ten Thousand Year Calendar for the accurate transition dates for each year.

| Day Master | Bing 丙 Fire | Month | Si 巳 (Snake) |

日元 Day Master	月 Month
丙 *Bing* **Yang Fire**	巳 *Si* **Snake** **Yin Fire**

For a Bing Fire Day Master born in a Si (Snake) Month, the Earthly Branch of Si (Snake) is Bing Fire's 'Prosperous' position. The absolute Thriving Structure is formed.

Where Bing Fire is revealed as one of the Heavenly Stems, a Thriving Structure is formed.

Where Wu Earth is revealed as one of the Heavenly Stems, an Eating God Structure may be formed when the conditions are completely met and supported by the Earthly branches.

Where Geng Metal is revealed as one of the Heavenly Stems, an Indirect Wealth Structure may be formed when the conditions are completely met and supported by the Earthly branches.

Day Master	Bing 丙 Fire		Month	Si 巳 (Snake)

喜用神提要 Regulating Useful God Reference Guide

月 Month	用神 Useful God

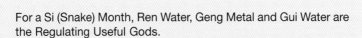

4th Month 四月 Si 巳 (Snake) Month	壬 Ren Yang Water	庚 Geng Yang Metal	癸 Gui Yin Water

Snake

For a Si (Snake) Month, Ren Water, Geng Metal and Gui Water are the Regulating Useful Gods.

Geng Metal is the secondary Useful God to this Day Master.

It is undesirable to have Wu Earth exerting an overly strong control over Ren Water – which is this Day Master's primary Useful God.

In the absence of Ren Water, Gui Water may be employed as a Useful God in its stead.

BaZi Structures & Structural Useful Gods 格局與格局用神

Day Master	Bing 丙 Fire	Month	Si 巳 (Snake)

6th day of May – 5th day of June, Gregorian Calendar

Where Jia Wood – this Day Master's Eating God Star – is also strong, Metal and Water would invariably be 'dry' and weak. Where Geng Metal is revealed, this person would enjoy a prosperous life.

There is, however, the need to avoid having additional Fire Qi countering and weakening Metal. Likewise, there is also the danger of Earth countering Water.

It is undesirable for this Day Master to encounter further Wood Qi as well. Where Fire is in abundance, this Day Master would be overly strong.

| Day Master | Bing 丙 Fire | Month | Si 巳 (Snake) |

Commentary

In addition to the preceding narratives on the potential Structures and scenarios resulting from a Bing Fire Day Master born in a Si (Snake) Month, the following circumstances also play their respective roles in determining the overall strength of this Day Master's BaZi Chart.

Snake

Note:

- Priority should be accorded to Ren Water, as this Day Master's primary Useful God. It would be all the better, should Ren Water also happen to be rooted in the Shen (Monkey) Earthly Branch. There is, however, the need to avoid having the Hai (Pig) and Si (Snake) Earthly Branches from clashing with one another, should the former also happen to be present in the BaZi Chart.

- Where Ren Water is missing from the Heavenly Stems, this person may lack support and drive to succeed in life.

- Even if Ren Water is present, Geng Metal must also be revealed in the Heavenly Stems.

- Where both Ren Water and Geng Metal are revealed – but Wu Earth and Ji Earth do not penetrate to the Heavenly Stems – this Day Master shall enjoy immense success in life.

- Where Ren Water is employed as a Useful God, it would also be preferable to have at least one Shen (Monkey) Earthly Branch present. Shen (Monkey) Earthly Branch is preferred to its Hai (Pig) counterpart, in bringing about more favorable outcomes to this Day Master.

- Where Gui Water substitutes for the absence of Ren Water – and while Bing Fire and Gui Water are both revealed in the Heavenly Stems – this Day Master may only be able to attain a modest level of success and wealth in life, at best.

- Where both Ren Water and Gui Water are missing, this Day Master may only be able to lead an average life, at best. He or she will also have to toil and slog in order to make an honest living.

- Where Wu Earth and Ji Earth are revealed in the Heavenly Stems, not only will this Day Master's career and relationship luck be poor; he or she may also be afflicted by poor health throughout life – and probably not be blessed with longevity, either.

- Where Wood and Fire Structures are formed in the BaZi Chart, Water must also be present. Otherwise, the overly strong presence of Fire may lead to this Day Master finding it hard to gain support or assistance, no matter what he or she does in life. And as a consequence, he or she may be plagued by loneliness and misery throughout his or her entire life.

- Where Metal (Wealth Star) is revealed – but Companion (Friend and Rob Wealth) Stars are not seen in the Heavenly Stems – this Day Master shall prosper and become wealthy in life. Should any Companion Stars happen to be revealed, however, this Day Master may be afflicted by poverty in life.

- Where Ren Water is missing and the Bing Fire sits on a Wu (Horse) Branch, a neagtive Goat Blade Star is formed. Under such circumstances, this Day Master may lack scruples and principles in life, and be even prone towards committing mischief or wrongdoing.

- Where Ji Earth is present and is keeping Ren Water under control, this Day Master may possess a despicable personality.

四月 Fourth Month

Snake

Day Master	Bing 丙 Fire	Month	Si 巳 (Snake)

Additional Attributes

格局 Structural Star	偏財 Indirect Wealth	七殺 Seven Killings
用神 Useful God	Geng 庚 Metal	Ren 壬 Water
Conditions	Presence of Geng Metal (Indirect Wealth Star) supporting Ren Water (Seven Killings) – the person shall prosper and become wealthy in life.	
Positive Circumstances	It would preferable for at least one Shen (Monkey) Earthly Branch to be present in the BaZi Chart.	
Negative Circumstances	Ji Earth contaminating Ren Water.	

格局 Structural Star	偏財 Indirect Wealth	正官 Direct Officer
用神 Useful God	Geng 庚 Metal	Gui 癸 Water
Conditions	With Geng Metal producing Gui Water – the person shall be able to become wealthy in life, albeit only to a certain extent; regardless of how intelligent he or she may be.	
Positive Circumstances	Geng Metal rooted in a Shen (Monkey) Earthly Branch.	
Negative Circumstances	Ji Earth in the Heavenly Stems.	

| Day Master | Bing 丙 Fire | | Month | Si 巳 (Snake) |

Additional Attributes

格局 **Structural Star**	偏財 Indirect Wealth
用神 **Useful God**	Geng 庚 Metal
Conditions	Geng Metal present helps support the Water Qi which is necessary for vitality of the chart.
Positive Circumstances	Geng Metal in the Heavenly Stems.
Negative Circumstances	Where the Earthly Branches form a Fire Structure with the Companion stars penetrating to the Heavenly Stems, this Day Master may be afflicted by poverty in life.

Snake

* *Ren Water is the primary Useful God to a Bing Fire Day Master born in a Si (Snake) Month.*

** *Geng Metal – as this Day Master's secondary Useful God – should not be missing, either.*

| Day Master | Bing 丙 Fire | Month | Si 巳 (Snake) |

Summary

- In the absence of Ren Water and Gui Water, not only will this Day Master be afflicted by poverty in life; indeed, he or she may also suffer from loneliness and lack of longevity.

- Where a Goat Blade Structure is formed, neither Jia Wood nor Yi Wood (both Resource Stars) may be used.

- With the formation of a Goat Blade Structure – the presence of Ren Water (Seven Killings Star) coupled with the absence of Wu Earth (Eating God Star) may cause this Day Master to not only be accident-prone, but also vulnerable to loneliness and depression in life.

Snake

Bing 丙 Fire Day Master, Born in Fifth Month 五月

Wu 午 (Horse) Month
June 6th - July 6th

Do note that the dates provided above are subject to slight yearly variations. Please refer to the Ten Thousand Year Calendar for the accurate transition dates for each year.

Horse

| Day Master Bing 丙 Fire | Month Wu 午 (Horse) |

日元 Day Master	月 Month
丙 Bing Yang Fire	午 Wu Horse Yang Fire

For a Bing Fire Day Master born in a Wu (Horse) Month, a Hurting Officer Structure is formed where Ji Earth is revealed as one of the Heavenly Stems.

Where Ding Fire is revealed as one of the Heavenly Stems, a Goat Blade Structure may be formed when the conditions are completely met and supported by the Earthly branches.

Day Master	Bing 丙 Fire	Month	Wu 午 (Horse)

喜用神提要 Regulating Useful God Reference Guide

月 Month	用神 Useful God
5th Month 五月 Wu 午 (Horse) Month	壬 Ren Yang Water 庚 Geng Yang Metal

Horse

For a Wu (Horse) Month, Ren Water and Geng Metal are the Regulating Useful Gods.

If Ren Water and Geng Metal are to be effective Useful Gods, however, both should preferably be rooted in the Shen (Monkey) Palace, as well.

BaZi Structures & Structural Useful Gods 格局與格局用神

Day Master	Bing 丙 Fire	Month	Wu 午 (Horse)

6th day of June – 6th day of July, Gregorian Calendar

Where a Goat Blade Structure is formed in this Day Master's BaZi Chart, Fire and Earth would be invariably too strong in the chart.

This is why it would be preferable for Metal and Water to be rooted in their respective elements – although their strengths, too, would be invariably weakened in the presence of such strong Fire and Earth. Where Water penetrates to the Heavenly Stems, the presence of Metal and Water in the Earthly Branches would certainly go a long way towards alleviating the preceding situation.

'Wet' or 'moist' Earth is the Medicating Useful God for a chart where Fire and Wood Qi happen to be strong. Only such Earth has the capacity to produce and strengthen Metal, while simultaneously weaken Fire.

Water represents the Spouse or Husband Star to female Bing Fire Day Masters. This is why Metal is needed to produce and ensure the continuity of Water.

Where Earth and Metal feature prominently in the case of male Day Masters, the latter shall be blessed with literary and penmanship skills. It would even be better if Water is encountered, as this would allow these Day Masters to also enjoy fame and fortune in life.

Day Master	Bing 丙 Fire	Month	Wu 午 (Horse)

Commentary

In addition to the preceding narratives on the potential Structures and scenarios resulting from a Bing Fire Day Master born in a Wu (Horse) Month, the following circumstances also play their respective roles in determining the overall strength of this Day Master's BaZi Chart.

Note:

- A best-case scenario for this Day Master would be where Ren Water and Geng Metal penetrate to the Heavenly Stems.

- It is undesirable to have Wu Earth, Ji Earth or Ding Fire penetrating to the Heavenly Stems, together with Geng Metal.

- The Wu (Horse) Earthly Branch contains Ding Fire and Ji Earth as its Hidden Stems. And Ji Earth, indirectly, is able to counter Water. This is why it would only be necessary to accord priority to Ren Water, as this Day Master's primary Useful God. There is also the need to avoid having Ji Earth penetrate to the Heavenly Stems. This is because Ji Earth 'contaminates' Ren Water, and combines with Jia Wood to form Earth.

- It is best to have Ren Water and Jia Wood revealed in the Heavenly Stems. In this scenario, there is the need to avoid having Geng Metal revealed and penetrating to the Heavenly Stems.

- Where only Ren Water is revealed – but Jia Wood is not – Geng Metal should preferably be revealed as well.

- Where Ding Fire and Ji Earth are both revealed and intermingle with one another in the Heavenly Stems, this Day Master may only be able to lead an average life at best; although he or she may also have to slog for a living.

- Where the Earthly Branches form a full Fire Structure – while Water is missing from the chart – this Day Master may lead a lonely, vagabond-like life.

- Where the Earthly Branches form a full Fire Structure – while Wu Earth and Ji Earth are revealed in the Heavenly Stems – Earth Qi would then divert the Fire. Under such circumstances, this Day Master may find assistance and support from friends and relatives hard to come by, more so in times of need.

- Where Metal and Water are missing from the chart, this Day Master shall find it extremely difficult to succeed in life.

Horse

| Day Master | Bing 丙 Fire | Month | Wu 午 (Horse) |

Additional Attributes

格局 Structural Star	七殺 Seven Killings	偏財 Indirect Wealth
用神 Useful God	Ren 壬 Water	Geng 庚 Metal
Conditions	Ideal to have Ren Water and one Geng Metal penetrate to the Heavenly Stems. Power and Wealth awaits for those who have this feature.	
Positive Circumstances	There is at least one Shen (Monkey) Earthly Branch present.	
Negative Circumstances	Wu Earth and Ji Earth penetrate to the Heavenly Stems – together with Ding Fire.	

五月 Fifth Month

Horse

| Day Master | Bing 丙 Fire | | Month | Wu 午 (Horse) |

Additional Attributes

五月 Fifth Month

格局 **Structural Star**	食神 Eating God	傷官 Hurting Officer
用神 **Useful God**	Wu 戊 Earth	Ji 己 Earth
Conditions	Where the Earthly Branches form a full Earth Structure, Ren Water and Jia Wood may be suitably employed as this Day Master's Useful Gods – and not Geng Metal and Ren Water.	
Positive Circumstances	Ren Water and Jia Wood in the Heavenly Stems.	
Negative Circumstances	Absence of Water element.	

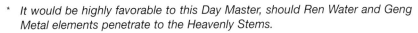

Horse

* *It would be highly favorable to this Day Master, should Ren Water and Geng Metal elements penetrate to the Heavenly Stems.*

** *Wu Earth, Ji Earth and Ding Fire should not penetrate to the Heavenly Stems.*

BaZi Structures & Structural Useful Gods 格局與格局用神

Day Master	Bing 丙 Fire	Month	Wu 午 (Horse)

Summary

- Where Water is missing from the chart, Metal should not be encountered either, in order for the overall structure of this Day Master's BaZi Chart to form a Follow Prosperous Structure.

Horse

Bing 丙 Fire Day Master, Born in Sixth Month 六月

Wei 未 (Goat) Month
July 7th - August 7th

Do note that the dates provided above are subject to slight yearly variations. Please refer to the Ten Thousand Year Calendar for the accurate transition dates for each year.

未
Goat

日元 Day Master	月 Month
丙 *Bing* **Yang Fire**	未 *Wei* **Goat** **Yin Earth**

For a Bing Fire Day Master born in a Wei (Goat) Month, a Hurting Officer Structure is formed where Ji Earth is revealed as one of the Heavenly Stems.

Where Yi Wood is revealed as one of the Heavenly Stems, a Direct Resource Structure is formed.

Where Ding Fire is revealed as one of the Heavenly Stems, a Thriving Structure may be formed when the conditions are completely met and supported by the Earthly branches.

Should, however, neither Yi Wood, Ding Fire nor Ji Earth happen to be revealed within the Heavenly Stems, one should select the BaZi Chart's most prominent Qi attribute at one's discretion.

Day Master	Bing 丙 Fire	Month	Wei 未 (Goat)

喜用神提要 Regulating Useful God Reference Guide

月 Month	用神 Useful God
6th Month 六月 Wei 未 (Goat) Month	壬 *Ren* **Yang Water**　　　庚 *Geng* **Yang Metal**

Goat

For a Wei (Goat) Month, Ren Water and Geng Metal are the Regulating Useful Gods.

Geng Metal serves as the auxiliary Useful God to this Day Master.

BaZi Structures & Structural Useful Gods 格局與格局用神

Day Master	Bing 丙 Fire	Month	Wei 未 (Goat)

7th day of July – 7th day of August, Gregorian Calendar

Although the Wei (Goat) Earthly Branch serves as storage for excess Wood Qi, Earth Qi nonetheless is dominant at this particular time of the year.

Fire would tend to be slightly weaker than Earth as it's Qi is channeled to Earth.

Water is used to provide 'moisture' and reduce the 'dryness' of Earth.

Goat

Wood Qi may be used to loosen the Earth.

It would, however, be unsuitable and unfavorable for this Day Master to encounter additional Earth Qi. This is because Earth 'contaminates' Water, as well as weakens Fire.

Where Fire and Earth are in abundance, Metal and Wood are needed to bring balance to this Day Master.

Day Master	Bing 丙 Fire		Month	Wei 未 (Goat)

六月 Sixth Month

Commentary

In addition to the preceding narratives on the potential Structures and scenarios resulting from a Bing Fire Day Master born in a Wei (Goat) Month, the following circumstances also play their respective roles in determining the overall strength of this Day Master's BaZi Chart.

Goat

Note:

- Geng Metal is the primary Useful God to this Day Master; with Ren Water as its secondary Useful God.

- Ji Earth should not penetrate to the Heavenly Stems.

- The criteria for determining Useful Gods in the case of a Bing Fire Day Master born in a Wei (Goat) Month is basically the same as the criteria used in Bing Fire born in a Wu (Horse) Month.

- In any case, neither Geng Metal nor Ren Water should be missing from the chart.

- This Day Master shall be able to lead a at minimum, a fairly good quality life, if not much better, where both Geng Metal and Ren Water are penetrated to the Heavenly Stems.

- It is undesirable having Ji Earth penetrate to the Heavenly Stems. This is because it has the capacity to 'contaminate' Ren Water – the Useful God.

- Where Ren Water is missing, this Day Master may suffer from a lack of intelligence and wisdom in life. The person may not be able to achieve stability despite much hard work and determination.

六月 Sixth Month

Goat

Day Master	Bing 丙 Fire		Month	Wei 未 (Goat)

Additional Attributes

格局 Structural Star	偏財 Indirect Wealth	七殺 Seven Killings
用神 Useful God	Geng 庚 Metal	Ren 壬 Water
Conditions	Both Geng Metal and Ren Water are revealed in the Heavenly Stems.	
Positive Circumstances	Where the Earthly Branches form a full Fire Structure, this Day Master shall prosper and enjoy immense good fortune.	
Negative Circumstances	Where Ji Earth penetrates to the Heavenly Stems, this Day Master may only lead an average life, at best.	

* Before the advent of 'Greater Heat' (Da Shu 大暑) from July 23rd to August 7th, it would be preferable to have two Ren Water and one Geng Metal elements as Useful Gods to this Day Master.

** After the advent of 'Greater Heat' (Da Shu 大暑), it would be preferable to have both Ren Water and Geng Metal present in parity – or similar strength – as Useful Gods to this Day Master.

Day Master	Bing 丙 Fire		Month	Wei 未 (Goat)

Summary

六月

Sixth Month

Goat

- Only Geng Metal and Ren Water may be suitably employed as Useful Gods to this Day Master.

- Without Geng Metal and Ren Water any structures formed may only be sub-pared at best.

- Where Ren Water is employed as the only Useful God, he or she would only find it favorable, when entering an Wood or Fire Luck cycles. It is only during 'reversed' or 'inverted' Luck Cycles that this Day Master will tend to do well.

- In ordinary settings, a Bing Fire Day Master born in a month other than Wei (Goat) would usually find it favorable when entering a Metal or Water Luck cycles.

Bing 丙 Fire Day Master, Born in Seventh Month 七月

Shen 申 (Monkey) Month
August 8th - September 7th

Do note that the dates provided above are subject to slight yearly variations. Please refer to the Ten Thousand Year Calendar for the accurate transition dates for each year.

七月 Seventh Month

Monkey

Day Master Bing 丙 Fire	Month Shen 申 (Monkey)

日元 Day Master	月 Month
丙 Bing Yang Fire	申 Shen Monkey Yang Metal

For a Bing Fire Day Master born in a Shen (Monkey) Month, an Indirect Wealth Structure is formed where Geng Metal is revealed as one of the Heavenly Stems.

Where Wu Earth is revealed as one of the Heavenly Stems, an Eating God Structure is formed.

Where Ren Water is revealed as one of the Heavenly Stems, a Seven Killings Structure is formed.

Should, however, neither Geng Metal nor Ren Water nor Wu Earth happen to be revealed amongst the Heavenly Stems, one should select a Structure according to the BaZi Chart's most prominent Qi attribute at one's discretion.

| Day Master | Bing 丙 Fire | Month | Shen 申 (Monkey) |

喜用神提要 **Regulating Useful God Reference Guide**

Monkey

月 Month	用神 Useful God
7th Month 七月 **Shen** 申 **(Monkey) Month**	壬 *Ren* **Yang Water** 戊 *Wu* **Yang Earth**

For a Shen (Monkey) Month, Ren Water and Wu Earth are the Regulating Useful Gods.

It would be ideal to have Ren Water rooted in the Shen (Monkey) Palace.

At the same time, if Ren Water is present in abundance, Wu Earth may be used to keep it under control.

BaZi Structures & Structural Useful Gods 格局與格局用神

Day Master	Bing 丙 Fire	Month	Shen 申 (Monkey)

8th day of August – 7th day of September, Gregorian Calendar

Monkey

Geng Metal is at its strongest, in the case of a Bing Fire Day Master born in a Shen (Monkey) Month. Metal and Water Qi are considered strong in this Month.

Where Metal Qi is present in abundance, Wood – the Resource Star – would invariably be weakened. Meanwhile, Fire and Earth – being weak – would also find it hard to keep Water, which is already strong, under control.

This is why Fire, Earth and Wood are needed as Useful Gods, since their combined support will bring balance to this Day Master, and allow it to become a 'sentimental' one.

Wood and Fire are especially needed as Useful Gods, especially where where Metal is vibrant – in order to 'protect' and ensure the sustenance of Bing Fire. 'Hot' Earth should also be present to prevent Water, being strong, from 'overflowing'.

| Day Master | Bing 丙 Fire | Month | Shen 申 (Monkey) |

Commentary

In addition to the preceding narratives on the potential Structures and scenarios resulting from a Bing Fire Day Master born in a Shen (Monkey) Month, the following circumstances also play their respective roles in determining the overall strength of this Day Master's BaZi Chart.

Note:

- Ren Water is the primary Useful God to a Day Master born in a Shen (Monkey) Month.

- It is undesirable to have Ji Earth should not penetrate to the Heavenly Stems.

- Ren Water must penetrate to the Heavenly Stems. For without which, the Bing Fire will not be able to realize it's full life potential.

- Where Wu Earth and Ji Earth are not seen or revealed in the Heavenly Stems, this Day Master would enjoy a good quality of life, especially when Ren Water is present.

- Where Wu Earth and Ji Earth are revealed in the Heavenly Stems, the overall Qi strength of this Day Master may be relatively weak.

- Thee presence of Friends Stars will add to the 'shine' and 'dazzle' of Bing Fire. Bing's Fire would be elegantly supported and allowed to 'shine' even more, by the presence of Ren Water. The general rule of thumb is simple: The stronger or more abundant Bing Fire's presence in the BaZi Chart, the better for this Day Master.

七
月

Seventh Month

Monkey

七月 Seventh Month

Monkey

| Day Master | Bing 丙 Fire | Month | Shen 申 (Monkey) |

Additional Attributes

格局 Structural Star	七殺 Seven Killings
用神 Useful God	Ren 壬 Water
Conditions	Ren Water, serving as favourable Seven Killings Star.
Positive Circumstances	The Wu Earth Hidden Stem contained within the Shen (Monkey) Earthly Branch may be used; but only if supported by Jia Wood (Indirect Resource Star).
Negative Circumstances	The Wu Earth Hidden Stem contained within the Chen (Dragon) and Wu (Horse) Earthly Branches should not be revealed, or penetrate to the Heavenly Stems.

Day Master	Bing 丙 Fire	Month	Shen 申 (Monkey)

Additional Attributes

Monkey

格局 Structural Star	偏財 Indirect Wealth
用神 Useful God	Geng 庚 Metal
Conditions	Where Geng Metal is present in the stems – and while Companion and Resource Stars remain missing from the chart – it would be possible for a Follow the Wealth Structure to be formed. Nevertheless, Geng Metal should not intermingle with Xin Metal (Direct Wealth Star), in order to achieve this purpose.
Positive Circumstances	Total absense of Companion and Resource stars to allow the chart to succeed in Follow the Wealth.
Negative Circumstances	Where a Follow the Wealth Structure is formed, neither Companion nor Resource Stars should be present.

* Ren Water is the primary Useful God for a Bing Fire Day Master born in a Shen (Monkey) Month.

** Resource (Direct and Indirect) and Companion (Friend and Rob Wealth) Stars should be present in the BaZi Chart, as well. They should also be rooted in the Yin (Tiger) and Si (Snake) Earthly branches.

BaZi Structures & Structural Useful Gods 格局與格局用神

Day Master	Bing 丙 Fire	Month	Shen 申 (Monkey)

Summary

Monkey

- It would be most suitable for Seven Killings and Resource Stars to be simultaneously applied in this chart.

- Where a Follow The Wealth Structure is successfully formed, Geng Metal is the main determinant, in deciding the quality of this structure. Nevertheless, it should not intermingle with the presence of Xin Metal.

- Where Geng Metal and Xin Metal are both present in the Heavenly Stems, it would not be possible for a true Follow the Wealth Structure to be formed.

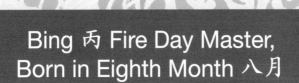

Bing 丙 Fire Day Master, Born in Eighth Month 八月

You 酉 (Rooster) Month
September 8th - October 7th

Do note that the dates provided above are subject to slight yearly variations. Please refer to the Ten Thousand Year Calendar for the accurate transition dates for each year.

BaZi Structures & Structural Useful Gods 格局與格局用神

| Day Master | Bing 丙 Fire | Month | You 酉 (Rooster) |

日元 Day Master	月 Month
丙 *Bing* **Yang Fire**	酉 *You* **Rooster** **Yin Metal**

For a Bing Fire Day Master born in a You (Rooster) Month, a Direct Wealth Structure is formed where Xin Metal is revealed as one of the Heavenly Stems.

Even if Xin Metal is not revealed as a Heavenly Stem, an Indirect Wealth Structure would still be considered to have been formed.

| Day Master | Bing 丙 Fire | Month | You 酉 (Rooster) |

喜用神提要 **Regulating Useful God Reference Guide**

八月 Eighth Month

Rooster

月 Month	用神 Useful God	
8th Month 八月 **You 酉 (Rooster) Month**	壬 *Ren* **Yang Water**	癸 *Gui* **Yin Water**

For a You (Rooster) Month, Ren Water and Gui Water are the Regulating Useful Gods.

Gui Water may be used to substitute Ren Water, in the absence of the latter.

BaZi Structures & Structural Useful Gods 格局與格局用神

| Day Master | Bing 丙 Fire | Month | You 酉 (Rooster) |

8th day of September – 7th day of October, Gregorian Calendar

Metal is at its strongest in autumn. The Yin Metal nature of the You (Rooster) Earthly Branch would also clash with Wood.

The strength of Wood Qi – the Resource Star – would be extremely limited. Water Qi is also very strong, this Month. And without Wood, it would be difficult for Bing Fire to 'shine' and 'brighten'.

As such, Wood and Fire are the secondary Useful Gods for this Day Master.

There is a need to avoid meeting Xin Metal as much as possible, since it weakens Wood, which is the Resource Star of Fire Qi.

八
月

Eighth Month

酉
Rooster

| Day Master | Bing 丙 Fire | | Month | You 酉 (Rooster) |

Commentary

In addition to the preceding narratives on the potential Structures and scenarios resulting from a Bing Fire Day Master born in a You (Rooster) Month, the following circumstances also play their respective roles in determining the overall strength of this Day Master's BaZi Chart.

Note :

- Ren Water is the primary Useful God to a Day Master born in a You (Rooster) Month.

- Ji Earth should not penetrate to the Heavenly Stems.

- Wood is needed as Useful Gods for this Day Master's vitality.

- The presence of Companion Stars will add to the 'shine' and 'dazzle' of Bing Fire. Ren Water will then elegantly support and allow to 'shine' even more. The stronger or more abundant Bing Fire's presence in the BaZi Chart, the better for this Day Master.

- Where Ji Earth is not seen or revealed in the Heavenly Stems, this Day Master would enjoy a good quality of life. This is to avoid having to contaminate the Ren Water.

- The Regulating Useful Gods for a Day Master born in a Shen (Monkey) Month and a Day Master born in a You (Rooster) Month are basically the same. The only difference lies in the fact that Friend Stars may be present in a You (Rooster) Month.

八
月

Eighth Month

Rooster

65

Day Master	Bing 丙 Fire	Month	You 酉 (Rooster)

Additional Attributes

格局 Structural Star	七殺 Seven Killings
用神 Useful God	Ren 壬 Water
Conditions	Both Resource and Friend Stars should also be present, along with Ren Water.
Positive Circumstances	-
Negative Circumstances	Presence of Wu Earth or Ji Earth penetrated to the Heavenly Stems.

| Day Master | Bing 丙 Fire | Month | You 酉 (Rooster) |

Additional Attributes

八月

Eighth Month

格局 Structural Star	正財 Direct Wealth
用神 Useful God	Xin 辛 Metal
Conditions	Xin Metal (Direct Wealth Star) penetrates to the Heavenly Stems. Under such circumstances, however, this Day Master may be afflicted by poverty, even after having made his or her fortune in life, earlier.
Positive Circumstances	Xin Metal separated from Bing Fire.
Negative Circumstances	Xin Metal combining with Bing Fire. Absence of Ding Fire.

酉

Rooster

* Ren Water is the primary Useful God for a Bing Fire Day Master born in a You (Rooster) Month.

** Wu Earth, Ji Earth and Xin Metal should not penetrate to the Heavenly Stems, either.

67

八月

Eighth Month

酉
Rooster

| Day Master | Bing 丙 Fire | Month | You 酉 (Rooster) |

Summary

- Where Gui Water is revealed this Day Master may prosper and become wealthy – although his or her wealth may not be sustainable.

- Where Xin Metal (Direct Wealth Star) is revealed – and Ding Fire (Rob Wealth Star) is also revealed in the Heavenly Stems – this Day Master may possess an unpredictable or 'unstable' character. The person may be solitary and indulge in sexual activities. He/she may achieve wealth earlier in life only to loose it towards the end.

- Where Xin Metal is present in abundance and competes with one another to combine to Bing Fire– he or she may be afflicted by poverty, chaos and obstructions in the latter or senior stages of his or her life.

- Where one Bing Fire and one Xin Metal combine with each other to form Water – while the Earthly Branches form a full Metal Structure, and neither Friend nor Rob Wealth Stars are revealed – this Day Master shall be privileged enough to enjoy the best possible quality of life. Under this condition, a special Transforming Qi Structure may have been formed.

Bing 丙 Fire Day Master, Born in Ninth Month 九月

Xu 戌 (Dog) Month
October 8th - November 6th

Do note that the dates provided above are subject to slight yearly variations. Please refer to the Ten Thousand Year Calendar for the accurate transition dates for each year.

BaZi Structures & Structural Useful Gods 格局與格局用神

| Day Master | Bing 丙 Fire | Month | Xu 戌 (Dog) |

日元 Day Master	月 Month
丙 *Bing* **Yang Fire**	戌 *Xu* **Dog** **Yang Earth**

For a Bing Fire Day Master born in a Xu (Dog) Month, an Eating God Structure is formed where Wu Earth is revealed as one of the Heavenly Stems.

Where Xin Metal is revealed as one of the Heavenly Stems, a Direct Wealth Structure is formed.

Where Ding Fire is revealed as one of the Heavenly Stems, a Goat Blade Structure may be formed when the conditions are completely met and supported by the Earthly branches.

Should, however, neither Wu Earth, Xin Metal nor Ding Fire happen to be revealed amongst the Heavenly Stems, one should select a Structure according to the BaZi Chart's most prominent Qi attribute at one's discretion.

| Day Master | Bing 丙 Fire | Month | Xu 戌 (Dog) |

喜用神提要 Regulating Useful God Reference Guide

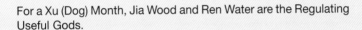

月 Month	用神 Useful God
9th Month 九月 Xu 戌 (Dog) Month	甲 *Jia* **Yang Wood** 　 壬 *Ren* **Yang Water**

Dog

For a Xu (Dog) Month, Jia Wood and Ren Water are the Regulating Useful Gods.

It is undesirable to have Earth – if prominently present - from stealing the shine of Bing Fire.

This is why Jia Wood is the primary Useful God, due to its ability to 'loosen' and keep Earth under control. Meanwhile, Ren Water serves as this Day Master's secondary Useful God.

BaZi Structures & Structural Useful Gods 格局與格局用神

| Day Master | Bing 丙 Fire | Month | Xu 戌 (Dog) |

8th day of October – 6th day of November, Gregorian Calendar

Earth is thick and leaden this month while Metal is cold.

Wood should not be missing from the chart. However, Wood faces the risk of becoming dry and parched. Hence, Water is also needed. Water and Wood are the most important Useful Gods to this Day Master.

Wood plays an important role 'loosening' Earth, this Month. It is also used to produce and strengthen Bing Fire. With Wood, the dry Earth would be able to be 'moistened' by the Water and serve as this Day Master's Useful God.

Dog

Metal is sought to produce Water – in the case where this chart's Fire is exceptionally strong and where Water is missing.

| Day Master | Bing 丙 Fire | Month | Xu 戌 (Dog) |

Commentary

In addition to the preceding narratives on the potential Structures and scenarios resulting from a Bing Fire Day Master born in a Xu (Dog) Month, the following circumstances also play their respective roles in determining the overall strength of this Day Master's BaZi Chart.

Dog

Note:

- Jia Wood is the primary Useful God to this Day Master, while Ren Water serves as its secondary Useful God.

- It is undesirable to have Ji Earth and Wu Earth to penetrate to the Heavenly Stems.

- Where both Ren Water and Jia Wood are revealed in the Heavenly Stems – and while Ji Earth does not penetrate to the Heavenly Stems – this Day Master shall be blessed with a fabulous career and wealth luck in life.

- Where Ren Water is not revealed in the Heavenly Stems (but Gui Water is) – with Jia Wood and Bing Fire also seen penetrating to the Heavenly Stems – this Day Master may also enjoy unexpected success in life.

- Where Ren Water and Geng Metal are both revealed in the Heavenly Stems – but Geng Metal counters Jia Wood – this Day Master may only be able to lead an average life at best; no matter how knowledgeable or learned he or she may be.

- Where Fire and Earth are present in abundance in the BaZi Chart, this Day Master may be compelled to travel or wander from place to place, in order to eke a living. He or she may also find it difficult to find a suitable life-partner, as well as remain on a long-term basis in a particular place.

- Where Ji Earth is revealed in the Heavenly Stems, but Jia Wood remains missing, this Day Master may lack a sense of purpose or direction in life. He or she may only lead an average life, at best.

BaZi Structures & Structural Useful Gods 格局與格局用神

Day Master Bing 丙 Fire	**Month** Xu 戌 (Dog)

Additional Attributes

格局 **Structural Star**	七殺 Seven Killings	偏印 Indirect Resource
用神 **Useful God**	Ren 壬 Water	Jia 甲 Wood
Conditions	Ren Water is used to produce Jia Wood.	
Positive Circumstances	Ren Water and Jia Wood rooted in the Branches and penetrated to the Heavenly Stems.	
Negative Circumstances	Geng Metal (Indirect Wealth Star) and and or Wu Earth (Eating God Star) penetrate to the Heavenly Stems.	

格局 **Structural Star**	食神 Eating God
用神 **Useful God**	Wu 戊 Earth
Conditions	Where Geng Metal and Xin Metal (Wealth Stars) are not or seen this Day Master may be afflicted by loneliness in life.
Positive Circumstances	Geng Metal, Xin Metal, Ren Water or Gui Water penetrate to the Heavenly Stems.
Negative Circumstances	Metal and Water are not revealed in the Heavenly Stems.

| Day Master | Bing 丙 Fire | Month | Xu 戌 (Dog) |

Additional Attributes

格局 Structural Star	傷官 Hurting Officer
用神 Useful God	Ji 己 Earth
Conditions	Where Ji Earth is penetrated to the Heavenly Stems but Jia Wood is not– this Day Master may lack a sense of purpose or direction in life.
Positive Circumstances	Jia Wood (Indirect Resource Star) penetrates to the Heavenly Stems.
Negative Circumstances	Ji Earth next to Ren Water.

Dog

*   Jia Wood – duly supported by Ren Water – is the primary Useful God to a Bing Fire Day Master born in a Xu (Dog) Month.

** this Day Master should avoid encountering Ji Earth.

九
月

Ninth Month

Day Master	Bing 丙 Fire	Month	Xu 戌 (Dog)

Summary

- Yi Wood cannot substitute Jia Wood, as a Useful God to this Day Master.

- Where Geng Metal, Xin Metal, Ren Water and or Gui Water are not revealed in the Heavenly Stems – with the presence of the Four Storage Earthly Branches of Chen (Dragon), Xu (Dog), Chou (Ox) and Wei (Goat) – this Day Master may be afflicted by poverty in life.

戌
Dog

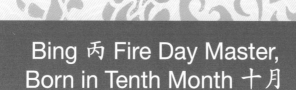

Bing 丙 Fire Day Master, Born in Tenth Month 十月

Hai 亥 (Pig) Month
November 7th - December 6th

Do note that the dates provided above are subject to slight yearly variations. Please refer to the Ten Thousand Year Calendar for the accurate transition dates for each year.

| Day Master | Bing 丙 Fire | Month | Hai 亥 (Pig) |

日元 Day Master	月 Month
丙 *Bing* **Yang Fire**	亥 *Hai* **Pig** **Yin Water**

For a Bing Fire Day Master born in a Pig (Hai) Month, a Seven Killings Structure is formed where Ren Water is revealed as one of the Heavenly Stems.

Where Jia Wood is revealed as one of the Heavenly Stems, an Indirect Resource Structure is formed.

Should, however, neither Ren Water nor Jia Wood happen to be revealed amongst the Heavenly Stems, one should select a Structure according to the BaZi Chart's most prominent Qi attribute at one's discretion.

Day Master	Bing 丙 Fire		Month	Hai 亥 (Pig)

喜用神提要 **Regulating Useful God Reference Guide**

Pig

月 **Month**	用神 **Useful God**
10th Month 十月 **Hai** 亥 **(Pig) Month**	甲 *Jia* Yang Wood 戊 *Wu* Yang Earth 庚 *Geng* Yang Metal 壬 *Ren* Yang Water

For a Hai (Pig) Month, Jia Wood, Wu Earth, Geng Metal and Ren Water are the Regulating Useful Gods.

Water is at its strongest, this Month. As such, Jia Wood may be used to keep it under control while supporting Bing Fire.

In a similar vein, Wu Earth may be employed to keep these elements under control.

Jia Wood is hence used to keep strong Water under control; while Geng Metal is used to keep strong Wood under control and generate Fire.

BaZi Structures & Structural Useful Gods 格局與格局用神

Day Master	Bing 丙 Fire	Month	Hai 亥 (Pig)

7th day of November – 6th day of December, Gregorian Calendar

Water is dominant in a Hai (Pig) Month. Wood Qi is secondary.

Given the Qi and timing of the month, sunlight – which also represents Bing Fire – is slowly losing its 'shine', as the days become gradually darker. And although the Hai (Pig) Earthly Branch contains Jia Wood as one of its Hidden Stems, it would still be impossible for 'wet' Wood to produce Fire.

Wood and Fire are hence the most important Useful Gods to this Day Master.

Metal may only be used where Wood and Fire happen to be severely strong in the chart. It would also be favorable for this Day Master, should Wealth and Officer Stars also happen to be present in sufficient strength.

Day Master	Bing 丙 Fire		Month	Hai 亥 (Pig)

Commentary

In addition to the preceding narratives on the potential Structures and scenarios resulting from a Bing Fire Day Master born in a Hai (Pig) Month, the following circumstances also play their respective roles in determining the overall strength of this Day Master's BaZi Chart.

Note:

- Jia Wood is the primary Useful God to this Day Master, while Ren Water is its secondary Useful God.

- It is undesirable to have Ji Earth penetrating to the Heavenly Stems.

- Where this Day Master meets Xin Metal (Direct Wealth Star) a transformation to Water may take place. Where the surrounding chart conditions support this transformation, this chart will belong to an extraordinary person.

- Where Jia Wood is present in abundance throughout the chart and revealed in the Heavenly Stems, Geng Metal must also be present in the BaZi Chart; in order that this Day Master may prosper and become wealthy in life.

| Day Master | Bing 丙 Fire | Month | Hai 亥 (Pig) |

Additional Attributes

格局 Structural Star	正財 Direct Wealth
用神 Useful God	Xin 辛 Metal
Conditions	Where Xin Metal (Direct Wealth Star) combines with Bing Fire and transform into Water – there must be at least one Chen (Dragon) Earthly Branch present in the BaZi Chart.
Positive Circumstances	Full support from surrounding circumstances to support the transformation.
Negative Circumstances	Jia Wood is present, but Wu Earth is missing.

十月 Tenth Month

亥 Pig

Day Master	Bing 丙 Fire		Month	Hai 亥 (Pig)

Additional Attributes

格局 Structural Star	七殺 Seven Killings	正官 Direct Officer
用神 Useful God	Ren 壬 Water	Gui 癸 Water
Conditions	A Follow the Killings Structure can only be formed when there is total absence of Ji Earth from the chart.	
Positive Circumstances	Follow The Killings is successfully formed.	
Negative Circumstances	Presence of Ji Earth and Fire Qi.	

Pig

* Jia Wood, Wu Earth and Geng Metal are the preferred Useful Gods for a Bing Fire Day Master born in a Hai (Pig) Month.

BaZi Structures & Structural Useful Gods 格局與格局用神

| Day Master | Bing 丙 Fire | Month | Hai 亥 (Pig) |

Summary

- Where Jia Wood is in abundance, Geng Metal (Indirect Wealth Star) is required, in order to keep Jia Wood under control.

- Without any Wealth Stars present in the BaZi Chart, this Day Master may only be able to lead an average life, at best.

- Where Ren Water is used, Wu Earth (Eating God Star) is required, in order to keep Ren Water under control.

亥
Pig

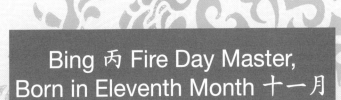

Bing 丙 Fire Day Master, Born in Eleventh Month 十一月

Zi 子 (Rat) Month
December 7th - January 5th

Do note that the dates provided above are subject to slight yearly variations. Please refer to the Ten Thousand Year Calendar for the accurate transition dates for each year.

十一月

Eleventh Month

Rat

| Day Master | Bing 丙 Fire | Month | Zi 子 (Rat) |

日元 Day Master	月 Month
丙 *Bing* **Yang Fire**	子 *Zi* **Rat** Yang Water

For a Bing Fire Day Master born in a Zi (Rat) Month, a Direct Officer Structure is formed where Gui Water is revealed as one of the Heavenly Stems.

Even if Gui Water is not revealed as a Heavenly Stem, a Seven Killings Structure would still be considered to have been formed.

Rat

Day Master	Bing 丙 Fire		Month	Zi 子 (Rat)

喜用神提要 **Regulating Useful God Reference Guide**

月 Month	用神 Useful God
11th Month 十一月 Zi 子 (Rat) Month	壬 戊 己 *Ren* *Wu* *Ji* **Yang Water** **Yang Earth** **Yin Earth**

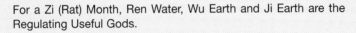

For a Zi (Rat) Month, Ren Water, Wu Earth and Ji Earth are the Regulating Useful Gods.

Ren Water is the primary Useful God to this Day Master, while Wu Earth may be used to keep Ren Water under control. Together, both allow this Bing Fire Day Master to transform from a weak to stronger one.

Meanwhile, Ji Earth may be used to substitute for Wu Earth, in the latter's absence.

Day Master Bing 丙 Fire	**Month** Zi 子 (Rat)

7th day of December – 5th day of January, Gregorian Calendar

Water is inevitably cold and possibly frozen into ice, in a Zi (Rat) Month – just as Wood would be, too. Under such circumstances, Bing Fire is 'isolated', without any help present within the immediate vicinity.

This is why 'hot' or 'fiery' Wood is needed. This means Wood harboring Fire Qi is needed in order to bring 'warmth' to an otherwise chilly scene. Such Wood will also produce and ensure the continuity of Fire.

Needless to say, without Wood and Fire Qi, it would be rather impossible for Bing Fire to 'shine' and retain at least a shred of 'brightness' at this time of the year by itself.

Since Metal, however counters and weakens Wood and produces Water; it would be preferable for this Day Master to avoid meeting Metal Qi as much as possible.

Meanwhile, 'hot' Earth may be used to keep Water under control. Furthermore, the presence and support of Wood would also go a long way in producing and ensuring the continuity of Fire.

Day Master	Bing 丙 Fire	Month	Zi 子 (Rat)

Commentary

In addition to the preceding narratives on the potential Structures and scenarios resulting from a Bing Fire Day Master born in a Zi (Rat) Month, the following circumstances also play their respective roles in determining the overall strength of this Day Master's BaZi Chart.

Note:

- Ren Water is the primary Useful God to this Day Master, while Wu Earth is its secondary Useful God. Where both are present, there would be no need for Jia Wood.

- Wu Earth is used to keep Water – which is strong in a Zi (Rat) Month – under control, when Jia Wood is missing from chart.

- Otherwise, where present, Jia Wood is should not be without Ding Fire, Wu Earth or Ren Water.

- Where Ding Fire is parted from Jia Wood, this Day Master may find it difficult to prosper in life. Jia Wood is need only because of the risk of Earth being overly 'leaden' or 'thick'.

- Where Wu Earth and Ji Earth – together with Ren Water – are revealed in the Heavenly Stems, but Jia Wood is not, this Day Master would belong to a scholarly person who is learned and knowledgeable.

- Where Ren Water is present but kept under control by Wu Earth - this is a conflict of Useful Gods. This denotes the possibility that the person may only succeed in the literary or scholastic fields. He or she may, however, may only enjoy limited success if life.

- There would be no need for Ren Water to be revealed in the Heavenly Stems, if the Earthly Branches forms a Fire Structure.

十一月 Eleventh Month

Rat

BaZi Structures & Structural Useful Gods 格局與格局用神

Day Master Bing 丙 Fire		Month Zi 子 (Rat)
Additional Attributes		

格局 **Structural Star**	七殺 Seven Killings	食神 Eating God
用神 **Useful God**	Ren 壬 Water	Wu 戊 Earth
Conditions	Wu Earth (Eating God) Star keeps Ren Water (Seven Killings Star) under control.	
Positive Circumstances	Wood (Resource Star) should not be missing, in order to produce and strengthen Bing Fire.	
Negative Circumstances	Ren Water (Seven Killings Star) is found in the Earthly Branches. And it forms a full Water Structure there along with other Branches. Under such circumstances, this Day Master may only enjoy very limited and short lived success in life.	

* Ren Water is the primary Useful God for a Bing Fire Day Master born in a Zi (Rat) Month.

** Wu Earth and Ji Earth are this Day Master's secondary Useful Gods.

| Day Master | Bing 丙 Fire | Month | Zi 子 (Rat) |

Summary

- In order for a Follow the Killings Structure to be formed in this Day Master's BaZi Chart, Wood (Resource Star) should not be present within the chart.

- Where Wood and Fire are present in abundance in the Earthly Branches, Ren Water (Seven Killings Star) may be used to ensure this Day Master remains well-balanced.

- Where Water is present in abundance in the Earthly Branches, Wu Earth (Eating God Star) may be used to keep Water under control.

Rat

Bing 丙 Fire Day Master, Born in Twelfth Month 十二月

Chou 丑 (Ox) Month
January 6th - February 3rd

Do note that the dates provided above are subject to slight yearly variations. Please refer to the Ten Thousand Year Calendar for the accurate transition dates for each year.

| Day Master | Bing 丙 Fire | Month | Chou 丑 (Ox) |

日元 Day Master	月 Month
丙 *Bing* **Yang Fire**	丑 *Chou* **Ox** **Yin Earth**

For a Bing Fire Day Master born in a Chou (Ox) Month, a Hurting Officer Structure is formed where Ji Earth is revealed as one of the Heavenly Stems.

Where Xin Metal is revealed as one of the Heavenly Stems, a Direct Wealth Structure is formed.

Where Gui Water is revealed as one of the Heavenly Stems, a Direct Officer Structure is formed.

Should, however, neither Ji Earth, Gui Water nor Xin Metal happen to be revealed amongst the Heavenly Stems, one should select a Structure according to the BaZi Chart's most prominent Qi attribute at one's discretion.

| Day Master | Bing 丙 Fire | Month | Chou 丑 (Ox) |

喜用神提要 Regulating Useful God Reference Guide

月 Month	用神 Useful God	
12th Month 十二月 Chou 丑 (Ox) Month	壬 *Ren* **Yang Water**	甲 *Jia* **Yang Wood**

十二月 Twelfth Month

丑 Ox

For a Chou (Ox) Month, Ren Water and Jia Wood are the Regulating Useful Gods.

Ren Water is the primary and hence most-preferred Useful God to this Day Master.

Where Earth is present in abundance, however, Jia Wood should not be lacking or missing, in order to keep Earth under control.

| Day Master | Bing 丙 Fire | Month | Chou 丑 (Ox) |

6th day of January – 3rd day of February, Gregorian Calendar

In a Chou (Ox) Month, Water – being strong - would make wet, icy and cold Earth, which in turn, would weaken the Qi of Bing Fire.

In addition, Wood – Resource Star – would also be wet and cold and hence unable to help produce and strengthen this Day Master. Indeed, the preceding circumstances would only result in an extremely weak Day Master.

This is why hot or warm Wood – rooted in its respective element - is needed as an important Useful God to this Day Master. It is only with the combined strength of Wood and Fire that Bing Fire – this Day Master's Self Element – may be produced and strengthened.

There is also the need for this Day Master to avoid meeting additional Metal and Water, as much as possible.

This is because Metal and Water have the capacity to counter and weaken the Qi of Bing Fire.

十二月

Twelfth Month

Ox

| Day Master | Bing 丙 Fire | Month | Chou 丑 (Ox) |

Commentary

Ox

In addition to the preceding narratives on the potential Structures and scenarios resulting from a Bing Fire Day Master born in a Chou (Ox) Month, the following circumstances also play their respective roles in determining the overall strength of this Day Master's BaZi Chart.

Note:

- Ren Water is the primary Useful God to this Day Master, while Jia Wood serves as its secondary Useful God.

- Where Ji Earth is seen penetrating to the Heavenly Stems, Jia Wood is also needed to keep it under control.

- As Bing Fire is Yang Fire, it would be possible for it to withstand the 'attack' by cold Qi of the month. Ren Water is needed as its primary Useful God to help the Bing Fire to shine.

- The Chou (Ox) Earthly Branch serves as storage for excess Earth and Metal Qi; the latter of which is this Day Master's Wealth Star. So, if either or both happen to be revealed in the Heavenly Stems, they should also be accompanied by Jia Wood to make them useable.

- Where Ren Water is employed as a Useful God to this Day Master, Ji Earth should not be allowed to 'contaminate' Ren Water. This is because while there is no risk of Bing Fire falling under the control of Ren Water, there is still the risk of Ji Earth weakening Bing Fire.

- And where Ren Water is employed as a Useful God, there is a need to prevent Ji Earth from 'contaminating' it.

- Ji Earth – being the proverbial 'Achilles' Heel' of this Day Master – should not penetrate to the Heavenly Stems; except when Xin Metal is also revealed in the chart. Metal weakens Earth. But take note that Xin Metal also has the tendency to combine with Bing Fire to form Water. This is why it is preferable and favorable for Jia Wood to also be revealed in the Heavenly Stems.

- Where Jia Wood remains hidden within the Earthly Branches, though, this Day Master may only be able to lead an average life, at best.

- Where Ji Earth is present in abundance in the Heavenly Stems, but Jia Wood and Yi Wood are totally missing, this would be an undesirable situation. This is because the Hurting Officer Star would be rather weak and superficial in strength this month and it would be impossible for a true Follow the Officer Structure to be formed. And even in the event that the special structure is indeed formed, it would only be superficial success in life; regardless of how brilliant or outstanding he or she may be.

- Where Ren Water is missing from the Heavenly Stems but Gui Water is instead present in abundance, there is also the possibility of having Gui Water countered and 'contaminated' by Ji Earth. Under such circumstances, this Day Master may not be able to prosper in life; despite his or her entrepreneurial spirit.

97

十二月 Twelfth Month

Ox

Day Master	Bing 丙 Fire	Month	Chou 丑 (Ox)

Additional Attributes

格局 Structural Star	七殺 Seven Killings	偏印 Indirect Resource
用神 Useful God	Ren 壬 Water	Jia 甲 Wood
Conditions	Where both Ren Water (Seven Killings Star) and Jia Wood (Indirect Resource Star) are present in strength, this Day Master shall enjoy success in his or her career-related pursuits. Should Jia Wood be missing but Ren Water present, this Day Master shall also prosper and become wealthy – albeit to a certain extent only.	
Positive Circumstances	This Day Master shall fare favourably in life, especially when entering a Wood or Fire Luck Period.	
Negative Circumstances	Absence of Ren Water.	

Day Master	Bing 丙 Fire	Month	Chou 丑 (Ox)

Additional Attributes

Ox

格局 Structural Star	傷官 Hurting Officer	正官 Direct Officer
用神 Useful God	Ji 己 Earth	Gui 癸 Water
Conditions	Where Ji Earth is in the Heavenly Stems – while Jia Wood and Yi happen to be missing – this Day Master may only enjoy superficial or limited success in life; regardless of how intelligent and outstanding he or she may be. Where both Ji Earth and Gui Water are seen penetrating to the Heavenly Stems simultaneously, this Day Master may fare better in life albeit having many health problems.	
Positive Circumstances	Jia Wood (Indirect Resource Star) is preferable to Yi Wood (Direct Resource Star), as a Useful God. Where Ji Earth and Gui Water penetrate to the Heavenly Stems together, Xin Metal should preferably be present as well – especially if this Day Master is to enjoy success in any entrepreneurial venture he or she undertakes in life.	
Negative Circumstances	Without Jia Wood or Yi Wood (Resource Stars), any Hurting Officer Structure formed would be a weak or superficial one.	

*   Ren Water and Jia Wood are the most-preferred Useful Gods for a Bing Fire Day Master born in a Chou (Ox) Month.

** Where Ji Earth is also employed as a Useful God, it should be supported by Jia Wood.

| Day Master | Bing 丙 Fire | Month | Chou 丑 (Ox) |

Summary

- When Ji Earth forms a Hurting Officer Structure with this Day Master – and while both the Resource Stars of Jia Wood and Yi Wood happen to be missing – any Hurting Officer Structure formed would still be a weak or superficial one.

- There is no need for Bing Fire to worry about being countered or controlled by Ren Water, – provided Wood is sufficiently present, to produce and ensure the continuity of Fire Qi.

- Should Ren Water happen to be missing from the chart, any structures formed would be sub pared.

- Without Jia Wood, it would be difficult – for this Day Master supported. It would be futile to use Companion Stars support and strengthen this Day Master should Jia Wood is missing.

Ding (丁) Fire
Day Master

Overview:

Ding 丁 Fire represents Yin Fire. Examples of Ding Fire include candlelight, as well as any other form of soft, gentle yet unyielding Fire.

Ding Fire Day Masters, due to their Yin nature, tend to be natural leaders and great motivators. They can also rise to the occasion when needed, and are meticulous, detail-oriented and sentimental by nature.

Do not be surprised, however, if a Ding Fire Day Master becomes de-motivated by him or herself – simply because this person was too busy igniting the proverbial fire in others, whilst forgetting to light his or her own fire.

To their credit, Ding Fire types are usually not the greedy type; especially once they have attained the level of wealth or success they have desired all along.

Insofar as Useful Gods are concerned, Jia Wood is the primary Resource Star and hence Useful God to a Ding Fire Day Master. Meanwhile, Geng Metal – another Useful God – is this Day Master's Direct Wealth Star. Working together, both Wood and Metal are the driving factors that determine that strength of Ding Fire Day Masters and hence, their corresponding outcomes in life.

Ding 丁 Fire Day Master, Born in First Month 正月

Yin 寅 (Tiger) Month
February 4th – March 5th

Do note that the dates provided above are subject to slight yearly variations. Please refer to the Ten Thousand Year Calendar for the accurate transition dates for each year.

| Day Master | Ding 丁 Fire | Month | Yin 寅 (Tiger) |

日元 Day Master	月 Month
丁 *Ding* **Yin Fire**	寅 *Yin* **Tiger** **Yang Wood**

For a Ding Fire Day Master born in a Yin (Tiger) Month, a Direct Resource Structure is formed where Jia Wood is revealed as one of the Heavenly Stems.

Where Wu Earth is revealed as one of the Heavenly Stems, a Hurting Officer Structure is formed.

Where Bing Fire is revealed as one of the Heavenly Stems, Goat Blade Structure may be formed when the conditions are completely met and supported by the Earthly branches.

Should, however, neither Jia Wood, Bing Fire nor Wu Earth happen to be revealed within the Heavenly Stems, one should select the BaZi Chart's most prominent Qi attribute at one's discretion.

Day Master	Ding 丁 Fire		Month	Yin 寅 (Tiger)

喜用神提要 **Regulating Useful God Reference Guide**

Tiger

月 Month	用神 Useful God
1st Month 正月 Yin 寅 (Tiger) Month	甲 *Jia* **Yang Wood**　　　庚 *Geng* **Yang Metal**

For a Yin (Tiger) Month, Jia Wood and Geng Metal are its Regulating Useful Gods.

Geng Metal should be used to keep Jia Wood under control, as well as 'conduct' the Qi of Ding Fire.

BaZi Structures & Structural Useful Gods 格局與格局用神

| Day Master | Ding 丁 Fire | | Month | Yin 寅 (Tiger) |

4th day of February – 5th day of March, Gregorian Calendar

Jia Wood is a Direct Resource Star to this Ding Fire Day Master. This Day Master still prefers to see Metal to cut the Wood and induce Fire.

In order to prevent transformation into a Fire Structure from taking place specially when Wood and Fire Qi are dominant in the chart, it requires Water to provide it with 'moisture'.

To achieve this end, Metal may be used to produce Water instead of controlling Wood.

In addition, it also helps to guard against having Ding Fire and Ren Water combine to form Wood.

Day Master	Ding 丁 Fire	Month	Yin 寅 (Tiger)

Commentary

In addition to the preceding narratives on the potential Structures and scenarios resulting from a Ding Fire Day Master born in a Yin (Tiger) Month, the following circumstances also play their respective roles in determining the overall strength of this Day Master's BaZi Chart.

Note:

Tiger

- Geng Metal and Ren Water are the Regulating Useful Gods for this Day Master.

- Jia Wood is strong in a Yin (Tiger) Month. This is why Geng Metal is needed to penetrate through the Heavenly Stems, in order to keep Jia Wood under control. Then and only then may Ren Water plays its role as a secondary Useful God.

- Jia Wood is a very strong Direct Resource to this Ding Fire Day Master this month. Geng Metal the Direct Wealth Star – may be used to produce Ren Water, which is this Day Master's Direct Officer Star.

- Where the Ren Water-Yin (Tiger) Hour Pillar appears in the BaZi Chart it may be possible for this Ding Fire and Ren Water to combine to form Wood. This transformation can only take place provided Geng Metal is not revealed in the chart.

- With Double Ren Water competing to combine with Ding Fire condition exists, Geng Metal must be revealed in the Heavenly Stems.

- Where Jia Wood is present in the Heavenly Stems and deeply rooted in the Earthly Branches, a rooted Geng Metal must also be seen in Heavenly Stems. In the absence of Geng Metal, this Day Master may be afflicted by poverty and poor health throughout his or her entire life.

- Where Jia Wood and Yi Wood (this Day Master's Resource Stars) are found in the Hidden Stems of all of the Earthly Branches - and in the absence of Geng Metal – this Day Master may be compelled to wander far and away in order to make a living. He or she may also find it very difficult to start a family or find companionship.

- Where the Earthly Branches form a full Fire Structure, and while Water is missing from the chart, this Day Master may be afflicted by loneliness and hardship in life.

Day Master	Ding 丁 Fire	Month	Yin 寅 (Tiger)

Additional Attributes

Tiger

格局 **Structural Star**	正官 Direct Officer
用神 **Useful God**	Ren 壬 Water
Conditions	Jia Wood is needed to penetrate to the Heavenly Stems should Ren Water be strong in this chart.
Positive Circumstances	Full Transformation of Qi takes place.
Negative Circumstances	Geng Metal is revealed in the Heavenly Stems.

格局 **Structural Star**	正官 Direct Officer	七殺 Seven Killings
用神 **Useful God**	Ren 壬 Water	Gui 癸 Water
Conditions	When Ren Water become too strong it will transform from Direct Officer to Seven Killings. Without Geng Metal, this Day Master may be afflicted by poverty, hardship, ailments in life.	
Positive Circumstances	Geng Metal (Indirect Wealth Star) penetrates through the Heavenly Stems.	
Negative Circumstances	Absence of Geng Metal.	

Day Master	Ding 丁 Fire	Month	Yin 寅 (Tiger)

Additional Attributes

格局 Structural Star	正印 Direct Resource	偏印 Indirect Resource
用神 Useful God	Jia 甲 Wood	Yi 乙 Wood
Conditions	Without Geng Metal (Indirect Wealth Star) penetrating through the Heavenly Stems, this Day Master may be afflicted by poverty in life. Where Yi Wood is present in abundance, this Day Master may also be inclined towards wandering aimlessly, no sense of purpose and direction throughout his or her entire life.	
Positive Circumstances	Geng Metal rooted and penetrating to the Heavenly Stems	
Negative Circumstances	Absence of Geng Metal	

Tiger

* *Geng Metal and Ren Water are the preferred Useful God for a Ding Fire Day Master born in a Yin (Tiger) Month.*

107

| Day Master | Ding 丁 Fire | Month | Yin 寅 (Tiger) |

Summary

- The presence of Geng Metal is vital to the survival of Ding Fire born in the Tiger Month. The quality and standard of life is determined by the quality of Geng Metal. Absence of Geng Metal would mean a substandard life.

正
月

First Month

Tiger

Ding 丁 Fire Day Master, Born in Second Month 二月

Mao 卯 (Rabbit) Month
March 6th – April 4th

Do note that the dates provided above are subject to slight yearly variations. Please refer to the Ten Thousand Year Calendar for the accurate transition dates for each year.

二月
Second Month

卯
Rabbit

| Day Master | Ding 丁 Fire | | Month | Mao 卯 (Rabbit) |

日元 Day Master	月 Month
丁 *Ding* **Yin Fire**	卯 *Mao* **Rabbit** **Yin Wood**

For a Ding Fire Day Master born in a Mao (Rabbit) Month, an Indirect Resource Structure is formed where Yi Wood is revealed as one of the Heavenly Stems.

Even if Yi Wood is not revealed as a Heavenly Stem, an Indirect Resource Structure would still be considered to have been formed.

Day Master	Ding 丁 Fire	Month	Mao 卯 (Rabbit)

喜用神提要 **Regulating Useful God Reference Guide**

月 **Month**	用神 **Useful God**	
2nd Month 二月 Mao 卯 (Rabbit) Month	庚 *Geng* **Yang Metal**	甲 *Jia* **Yang Wood**

Geng Metal and Jia Wood are its Regulating Useful Gods.

Geng Metal is used to keep Yi Wood under control.

Meanwhile, Jia Wood is used to produce and ensure the continuity of Ding Fire.

二月 Second Month

Rabbit

111

Second Month

二月

Rabbit

Day Master	Ding 丁 Fire	Month	Mao 卯 (Rabbit)

6ᵗʰ day of March – 4ᵗʰ day of April, Gregorian Calendar

Wood is the strongest at this time of the year. Metal should hence be chosen as the Useful God to keep strong Wood Qi under control. Meanwhile, Water may be used to provide 'moisture' as well as reduce the heat and dryness brought about by this Day Master.

Water, in a Mao (Rabbit) Month, does however have the ability to produce Wood.

A Day Master born in where Fire and Earth are prominently present would therefore require 'wet' or 'moist' Earth to weaken Fire, and also produce Metal.

Day Master	Ding 丁 Fire	Month	Mao 卯 (Rabbit)

Commentary

In addition to the preceding narratives on the potential Structures and scenarios resulting from a Ding Fire Day Master born in a Mao (Rabbit) Month, the following circumstances also play their respective roles in determining the overall strength of this Day Master's BaZi Chart.

Note:

- Geng Metal is the primary Useful God for a Ding Fire Day Master born in a Mao (Rabbit) Month, with Jia Wood serving as the secondary Useful God.

- It is undesirable for additional Fire element to penetrate to the Heavenly Stems.

- Where Geng Metal and Yi Wood appears side-by-side, a combination to produce Metal takes place. Where the combination is successful, an unfavorable outcome await. Hence, it is desirable for the person to go through Wood or Fire Luck as to prevent the Metal Qi from being produced. Where the person goes through Metal and Water cycles, life would be filled with obstacles, hassles and tribulations.

- It is undesirable for Yi Wood to be revealed in the Heavenly Stems. The person stands a higher chance for success in life when Yi Wood does not appear in the Heavenly Stems. With strong presence of Yi Wood, this person, even though may acquire some wealth during his lifetime but such wealth is not sustainable.

- Where Gui Water is revealed in the Heavenly Stems – but Ji Earth is missing from the chart– this Day Master may be afflicted by poverty and fear in life.

- It would be a best-case scenario for this Day Master, where the Earthly Branches form a full Fire Structure, while Geng Metal is revealed in the Heavenly Stems. Without Geng Metal, however, this Day Master may be afflicted by many difficulties, hardship and even poverty in life.

二
月

Second Month

Rabbit

113

Day Master	Ding 丁 Fire	Month	Mao 卯 (Rabbit)

Additional Attributes

格局 Structural Star	正財 Direct Wealth	正印 Direct Resource
用神 Useful God	Geng 庚 Metal	Jia 甲 Wood
Conditions	Where Geng Metal and Jia Wood are both revealed in the Heavenly Stems, this Day Master shall enjoy success in his or her career-related pursuits. Where Geng Metal is revealed but Jia Wood is not, this Day Master shall still belong to a learned, knowledgeable person albeit not very wealthy. Where Jia Wood is revealed but Geng Metal is not, this Day Master may only lead an average life at best.	
Positive Circumstances	It would be preferable for Gui Water to be revealed in the Heavenly Stems.	
Negative Circumstances	Ren Water appearing next to Ding Fire, forcing a combination to take place.	

格局 Structural Star	偏印 Indirect Resource
用神 Useful God	Yi 乙 Wood
Conditions	Yi Wood penetrates to the Heavenly Stems and combines with Geng Metal to form Metal. Where Yi Wood remains a Hidden Stem within the Earthly Branches, it would still be favorable to this Day Master. Where Yi Wood is present but Geng Metal missing, this Day Master may be afflicted by difficulties and poverty in life.
Positive Circumstances	Where Geng Metal is revealed but Yi Wood remains hidden, it would still be favourable to this Day Master when he or she enters a Wood or Fire Luck cycles.
Negative Circumstances	Where Yi Wood is revealed in the Heavenly Stems, this Day Master may be afflicted by poverty when entering a Metal or Water Luck Period.

Day Master	Ding 丁 Fire		Month	Mao 卯 (Rabbit)

Additional Attributes

卯
Rabbit

格局 Structural Star	七殺 Seven Killings
用神 Useful God	Gui 癸 Water
Conditions	Where Gui Water is revealed in the Heavenly Stem, Wu Earth (Hurting Officer Star) and or Ji Earth (Eating God Star) must also be present to keep Gui Water under control. Otherwise, this Day Master may be afflicted by a lack of purpose and self identity leading to poverty in life.
Positive Circumstances	Wu Earth and Ji Earth penetrate to the Heavenly Stems.
Negative Circumstances	Wu Earth and Ji Earth are not revealed.

格局 Structural Star	劫財 Rob Wealth	比肩 Friend
用神 Useful God	Bing 丙 Fire	Ding 丁 Fire
Conditions	Where Geng Metal is also present, this Day Master's BaZi Chart would be of a favourable structure. Indeed, without Geng Metal, the BaZi Chart would be of a substandard structure.	
Positive Circumstances	Geng Metal (a Direct Wealth Star) penetrates to the Heavenly Stems.	
Negative Circumstances	-	

* *Geng Metal and Jia Wood are the preferred Useful Gods for a Ding Fire Day Master born in a Mao (Rabbit) Month.*

Day Master Ding 丁 Fire

Month Mao 卯 (Rabbit)

二月 Second Month

Summary

- Yi Wood (Indirect Resource Star) should not be revealed or penetrate to the Heavenly Stems.

- Geng Metal (Direct Wealth Star) must, however, be present and available as a Useful God, if this Day Master is to succeed in life.

Rabbit

Ding 丁 Fire Day Master, Born in Third Month 三月

Chen 辰 (Dragon) Month
April 5th - May 5th

Do note that the dates provided above are subject to slight yearly variations. Please refer to the Ten Thousand Year Calendar for the accurate transition dates for each year.

| Day Master | Ding 丁 Fire | Month | Chen 辰 (Dragon) |

Dragon

日元 **Day Master**	月 **Month**
丁 *Ding* **Yin Fire**	辰 *Chen* **Dragon** **Yang Earth**

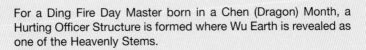

For a Ding Fire Day Master born in a Chen (Dragon) Month, a Hurting Officer Structure is formed where Wu Earth is revealed as one of the Heavenly Stems.

Where Yi Wood is revealed as one of the Heavenly Stems, an Indirect Resource Structure is formed.

Where Gui Water is revealed as one of the Heavenly Stems, a Seven Killings Structure is formed.

Should, however, neither Yi Wood nor Wu Earth nor Gui Water happen to be revealed within the Heavenly Stems, one should select a Structure according to the BaZi Chart's most prominent Qi attribute at one's discretion.

| Day Master | Ding 丁 Fire | Month | Chen 辰 (Dragon) |

喜用神提要 **Regulating Useful God Reference Guide**

三月 Third Month

月 Month	用神 Useful God
3rd Month 三月 Chen 辰 (Dragon) Month	甲 *Jia* **Yang Wood** 庚 *Geng* **Yang Metal**

Dragon

Ding Fire born in a Chen (Dragon) Month, Jia Wood and Geng Metal are its most important Regulating Useful Gods.

Jia Wood is used to produce Ding Fire and also keep Earth under control.

Geng Metal may then be used as a secondary Useful God where Wood is strong. Geng Metal should be used to keep wood Qi under control.

Likewise, where Water is strong, Wu Earth may be used to keep it under control.

119

BaZi Structures & Structural Useful Gods 格局與格局用神

Day Master	Ding 丁 Fire	Month	Chen 辰 (Dragon)

5th day of April – 5th day of May, Gregorian Calendar

The Chen (Dragon) Earthly Branch – contains the Hidden Stem of Wu Earth. This in turn weakens the Qi of Ding Fire, since Fire produces Earth. The best approach to mitigate the preceding situation would hence be to use Wood to keep Earth under control, as well as produce Fire.

This Day Master also has the potential to combine to form Wood. A successful transformation promises an extraordinary life. But this would greatly depend on the Hour Pillar's support.

Dragon

Where Wood is strong and with the presence of adequate Metal Qi, he or she shall prosper and become wealthy in life.

| Day Master | Ding 丁 Fire | Month | Chen 辰 (Dragon) |

Commentary

In addition to the preceding narratives on the potential Structures and scenarios resulting from a Ding Fire Day Master born in a Chen (Dragon) Month, the following circumstances also play their respective roles in determining the overall strength of this Day Master's BaZi Chart.

Dragon

Note:

- Jia Wood is the primary Useful God for a Ding Day Master born in a Chen (Dragon) Month, while Geng Metal serves as the secondary Useful God.

- Where Geng Metal and Jia Wood are both revealed in the Heavenly Stems, this Day Master shall lead a life of superior quality, wealth and comfort.

- Where the Yin (Tiger), Mao (Rabbit) and Chen (Dragon) Earthly Branches form a full Wood Structure, Geng Metal must also be seen or revealed in the Heavenly Stems. At the same time, it is undesirable to have Ding Fire (Friend Star) penetrating to the Heavenly Stems, since it exerts a control and harm over Geng Metal.

- Where the Shen (Monkey), Zi (Rat) and Chen (Dragon) Earthly Branches form a full Water Structure – and while Wu Earth and Ji Earth are not revealed in the Heavenly Stems – this Day Master may be afflicted by poverty and poor health in life.

- Where there is no Water Qi in the Earthly Branches, there would be no use for Wu Earth and Ji Earth.

三月 Third Month

辰 Dragon

Day Master	Ding 丁 Fire		Month	Chen 辰 (Dragon)

Additional Attributes

格局 Structural Star	正印 Direct Resource	正財 Direct Wealth
用神 Useful God	Jia 甲 Wood	Geng 庚 Metal
Conditions	Where Jia Wood and Geng Metal are both revealed, this Day Master shall enjoy success in his or her career-related pursuits.	
Positive Circumstances	Jia Wood and Geng Metal appearing in the Heavenly Stems.	
Negative Circumstances	Ding Fire (Friend Star) penetrates to the Heavenly Stems.	

| Day Master | Ding 丁 Fire | | Month | Chen 辰 (Dragon) |

Additional Attributes

格局 Structural Star	正官 Direct Officer	七殺 Seven Killings
用神 Useful God	Ren 壬 Water	Gui 癸 Water
Conditions	Where the Shen (Monkey), Zi (Rat) and Chen (Dragon) Earthly Branches form a full Water Structure – this Day Master shall prosper in life, if at the same time, Wu Earth and Ji Earth are also revealed in the Heavenly Stems. Where neither Wu Earth nor Ji Earth is revealed, this Day Master may not enjoy a life of quality.	
Positive Circumstances	Wu Earth and Ji Earth are both revealed in the Heavenly Stems. Should, however, only either one happen to be revealed, this Day Master may not be able to realise its full potential.	
Negative Circumstances	Wu Earth and Ji Earth are not revealed in the Heavenly Stems. Even if Wu Earth and Ji Earth happen to be revealed, it still will not do if Jia Wood is also in the Heavenly Stems.	

Dragon

* *Jia Wood and Geng Metal are the preferred Useful Gods for a Ding Fire Day Master born in a Chen (Dragon) Month.*

| Day Master | Ding 丁 Fire | Month | Chen 辰 (Dragon) |

三月 Third Month

Summary

- It would also be unfavorable for this Day Master should excessive water is formed in the chart.

- Only Wu Earth and Ji Earth can salvage an excessive Water Qi.

- Where Geng Metal or Xin Metal are present, this Day Master should also avoid encountering Gui Water (Seven Killings Star).

Dragon

Ding 丁 Fire Day Master, Born in Fourth Month 四月

Si 巳 (Snake) Month
May 6th - June 5th

Do note that the dates provided above are subject to slight yearly variations. Please refer to the Ten Thousand Year Calendar for the accurate transition dates for each year.

四
月 **Fourth Month**

Snake

| Day Master | Ding 丁 Fire | Month | Si 巳 (Snake) |

日元 **Day Master**	月 **Month**
丁 *Ding* **Yin Fire**	巳 *Si* **Snake** **Yin Fire**

For a Ding Fire Day Master born in a Si (Snake) Month, a Direct Wealth Structure is formed where Geng Metal is revealed as one of the Heavenly Stems.

Where Wu Earth is revealed as one of the Heavenly Stems, a Hurting Officer Structure is formed.

Where Bing Fire is revealed as one of the Heavenly Stems, Goat Blade Structure may be formed when the conditions are completely met and supported by the Earthly branches.

Should, however, neither Bing Fire, Wu Earth nor Geng Metal happen to be revealed within the Heavenly Stems, one should select a Structure according to the BaZi Chart's most prominent Qi attribute at one's discretion.

| Day Master | Ding 丁 Fire | Month | Si 巳 (Snake) |

喜用神提要 **Regulating Useful God Reference Guide**

四月 Fourth Month

月 **Month**	用神 **Useful God**
4th Month 四月 Si 巳 (Snake) Month	甲 *Jia* **Yang Wood** 庚 *Geng* **Yang Metal**

Snake

For a Si (Snake) Month, Jia Wood and Geng Metal are the Regulating Useful Gods.

Jia Wood may be used to produce and ensure the continuity of Ding Fire.

Where Jia Wood is present in abundance, Geng Metal should be employed as the primary Useful God to keep Jia Wood under control.

Water can also be chosen as a Regulating Useful God where moist is needed in this dry hot fire month.

Day Master Ding 丁 Fire	**Month** Si 巳 (Snake)

6th day of May – 5th day of June, Gregorian Calendar

Fire is obviously strong in the summer month. Metal and Water will consequently tend to be 'parched' or even 'dry' during this time.

As such, Water would first be needed to 'moisten' this Ding Fire Day Master.

The Geng Metal Hidden Stem found inside the Si (Snake) Earthly Branch may be selected as the Useful God, in order to produce and ensure the continuity of Water.

It is undesirable for this Day Master to further encounter Fire Qi. Wood should also be avoided, since it produces and strengthens Fire.

'Wet' or 'moistened' Earth would also aid this Day Master. It is only in its presence that Metal can be prevented from becoming overly 'dry'.

A Day Master born in an hour where Metal and Water Qi is strong would find it easier to have use the Metal stars met during the course of life in this BaZi Chart. Under such circumstances, this Day Master shall be blessed with fame and good fortune in life.

Day Master	Ding 丁 Fire		Month	Si 巳 (Snake)

Commentary

In addition to the preceding narratives on the potential Structures and scenarios resulting from a Ding Fire Day Master born in a Si (Snake) Month, the following circumstances also play their respective roles in determining the overall strength of this Day Master's BaZi Chart.

Note:

Snake

- Jia Wood and Geng Metal are the preferred Useful Gods for this Ding Fire Day Master.

- It is undesirable to have Gui Water penetrating to the Heavenly Stems. It can, however be seen inside the Earthly Branches.

- Fire Qi features prominently in a Si (Snake) Month. Where Bing Fire is revealed and penetrates to the Heavenly Stems, the Ren Water and Geng Metal are the preferred Useful Gods. This scenario is also known as Bing Fire 'stealing' or 'snatching' the 'luster' and 'shine' of Ding Fire. When this scenario happens, the Ding Fire person is always outshined by others.

- Where Wu Earth and Ji Earth are present in abundance – causing the overall Qi of this Day Master's BaZi Chart to become overly 'dry' and 'parched', Water Qi is invariably needed. Where this scenario is seen, this Day Master would belong to a learned, knowledgeable person. However, he or she may find it difficult to achieve fame and authority in life even with such high intelligence. Consequently this leads to discontentment in life.

- Where Yi Wood – Indirect Resource Star - is revealed in the Heavenly Stems, this Day Master may only lead an average life at best.

BaZi Structures & Structural Useful Gods 格局與格局用神

Day Master	Ding 丁 Fire		Month	Si 巳 (Snake)

Additional Attributes

Snake

格局 Structural Star	傷官 Hurting Officer	正財 Direct Wealth
用神 Useful God	Wu 戊 Earth	Geng 庚 Metal
Conditions	Where Wu Earth (Hurting Officer Star) successfully produces Metal (Wealth Star), this Day Master shall prosper and become immensely wealthy in life.	
Positive Circumstances	Presence of rooted Geng Metal in the chart.	
Negative Circumstances	Where Yi Wood is also revealed, this Day Master may only lead an average life, at best.	

Day Master Ding 丁 Fire	Month Si 巳 (Snake)

Additional Attributes

格局 **Structural Star**	劫財 Rob Wealth
用神 **Useful God**	Bing 丙 Fire
Conditions	Where Bing Fire penetrates to the Heavenly Stems in a summer month, Bing Fire would be considered to have 'stolen' or 'snatched' the 'shine' or 'lustre' of Ding Fire. Without Ren Water and Gui Water revealed as well, this Day Master may be afflicted by poverty in life. He or she may constantly feel outshine and outperformed by others.
Positive Circumstances	Ren Water and Gui Water penetrate to the Heavenly Stems. The best-case scenario would be to have Jia Wood and Bing Fire present a the same time.
Negative Circumstances	This Day Master enters a Metal or Water Luck Period.

Snake

* *Jia Wood and Geng Metal are the preferred Useful Gods for a Ding Fire Day Master born in a Si (Snake) Month.*

***Gui Water (Seven Killings Star) should be avoided at the Heavenly Stems, since it is this Day Master's proverbial 'Achilles' Heel'. It however would be acceptable to be found in the Earthly Branches. Bing Fire should not be revealed, either, since it has the potential to 'snatch' or 'steal' the 'shine' or 'luster' of Ding Fire.*

四
月

Fourth Month

| Day Master | Ding 丁 Fire | Month | Si 巳 (Snake) |

Summary

- Bing Fire should not be revealed in the Heavenly Stems, in the case of this Day Master. Otherwise, Ren Water and Gui Water must also be revealed in the Heavenly Stems.

- If Bing Fire is not revealed in the Heavenly Stems, Ren Water and Gui Water should preferably not penetrate to the Heavenly Stems as well.

Snake

Ding 丁 Fire Day Master, Born in Fifth Month 五月

Wu 午 (Horse) Month
June 6th - July 6th

Do note that the dates provided above are subject to slight yearly variations. Please refer to the Ten Thousand Year Calendar for the accurate transition dates for each year.

| Day Master | Ding 丁 Fire | Month | Wu 午 (Horse) |

日元 Day Master	月 Month
丁 Ding Yin Fire	午 Wu Horse Yang Fire

For a Ding Fire Day Master born in a Wu (Horse) Month, the Earthly Branch of Wu (Horse) is Ding Fire's 'Prosperous' position. Where Ding Fire is revealed as one of the Heavenly Stems, a Thriving Structure may be formed when the conditions are completely met and supported by the Earthly branches.

| Day Master | Ding 丁 Fire | Month | Wu 午 (Horse) |

喜用神提要 Regulating Useful God Reference Guide

月 Month	用神 Useful God
5th Month 五月 Wu 午 (Horse) Month	壬 *Ren* **Yang Water** 　 庚 *Geng* **Yang Metal** 　 癸 *Gui* **Yin Water**

Horse

For a Wu (Horse) Month, Ren Water, Geng Metal and Gui Water are the Regulating Useful Gods.

Where Water is present in abundance – and Geng Metal and Ren Water are both revealed – this Day Master shall enjoy immense prosperity in life.

In the absence of Ren Water, Gui Water may also be used in its stead. Nevertheless, it would not be as good, compared to Ren Water being present and available as a Useful God.

135

Day Master	Ding 丁 Fire	Month	Wu 午 (Horse)

6th day of June – 6th day of July, Gregorian Calendar

Ding Fire would be at its strongest in a Wu (Horse) Month.

This Day Master would obviously clash with - and counter - any Water it encounters. And given the immense strength of Fire, it would also 'melt' and weaken any Metal it encounters.

As such, both Metal and Water would have to be rooted in their respective elements; otherwise, they would not be able to bring balance to this Day Master.

A Day Master born in an hour where Wood and Fire are strong should also have 'wet' or 'moistened' Earth present as a Medicating Useful God. This is because 'wet' Earth produces and strengthens Metal, as well as weakens Fire, which is already too strong.

Water represents the Spouse or Husband Star to female Ding Fire Day Masters. This is why Metal is needed to produce and ensure the continuity of Water. There is also the need to be wary of Ding Fire and Ren Water combining to form Wood.

In addition, where additional Fire Qi is present in abundance, it would also be hard for Water to be sustained. Nevertheless, male Day Masters can still be blessed with fame and fortune in life under such circumstances, provided a successful thriving structure is formed.

| Day Master | Ding 丁 Fire | Month | Wu 午 (Horse) |

Commentary

In addition to the preceding narratives on the potential Structures and scenarios resulting from a Ding Fire Day Master born in a Wu (Horse) Month, the following circumstances also play their respective roles in determining the overall strength of this Day Master's BaZi Chart.

Note:

- Ren Water should preferably penetrate to the Heavenly Stems. The best-case scenario would be the have Ren Water found as the Heavenly Stem of the Month Pillar.

- Another favorable scenario would be for this Day Master to be born in a Hai (Pig) Hour, or have a Ding Fire-Hai (Pig) Day Pillar in the BaZi Chart.

- The positive attributes of the Ding Fire Heavenly Stem will be exerted depending on its relationship with Ren Water. It is undesirable, where Ren Water is the Useful God, to have Wu Earth and Ji Earth penetrating to the Heavenly Stems.

- Where Bing Fire appears in the Heavenly Stems, it would then 'steal' the 'shine' or 'luster' of Ding Fire. The person would encounter many instances where his or her life is outshined or outperformed by his friends or siblings.

  It would not be necessary for the Yin (Tiger), Wu (Horse) and Si (Snake) Earthly Branches to be all present, in order for a strong Fire Structure to be formed. Provided there are at least two or three Wu (Horse) Earthly Branches present in the BaZi Chart, a Fire Structure would be considered to have been formed.

五
月

Fifth Month

Horse

BaZi Structures & Structural Useful Gods 格局與格局用神

五月 Fifth Month

Horse

Day Master Ding 丁 Fire		**Month** Wu 午 (Horse)

Additional Attributes

格局 **Structural Star**	正財 Direct Wealth	正官 Direct Officer
用神 **Useful God**	Geng 庚 Metal	Ren 壬 Water
Conditions	Where both Geng Metal and Ren Water – the Direct Wealth and Direct Officer Stars – are both revealed, this Day Master shall enjoy enviable success in his or her career-related pursuits.	
Positive Circumstances	Geng Metal and Ren Water appearing in the Heavenly Stems.	
Negative Circumstances	Geng Metal remains hidden, while Ji Earth (Eating God Star) is revealed.	

格局 **Structural Star**	正印 Direct Resource	偏印 Indirect Resource
用神 **Useful God**	Jia 甲 Wood	Yi 乙 Wood
Conditions	Where the Hai (Pig) and Mao (Rabbit) Earthly Branches form a Wood Structure, this Day Master may only lead an average life at best. He or she may not be able to get along with his or her children as well.	
Positive Circumstances	Jia Wood appearing in the Heavenly Stems. Wet Earth is found in the chart.	
Negative Circumstances	Geng Metal is next to Yi Wood or Jia Wood.	

Day Master	Ding 丁 Fire		Month	Wu 午 (Horse)

五月

Fifth Month

Additional Attributes

格局 **Structural Star**	劫財 Rob Wealth
用神 **Useful God**	Bing 丙 Fire
Conditions	Where Bing Fire is revealed in the Heavenly Stems and 'steals' or 'snatches' the 'shine' or 'lustre' of Ding Fire. All the Earthly Branches are in support of the Fire.
Positive Circumstances	This Day Master enters a Wood or Fire Luck Period.
Negative Circumstances	This Day Master enters a Metal or Water Luck Period.

Horse

* *Geng Metal and Ren Water are the preferred Useful Gods for a Ding Fire Day Master born in a Wu (Horse) Month.*

Day Master	Ding 丁 Fire	Month	Wu 午 (Horse)

Summary

- Water is needed to keep the glare of Bing Fire under control. Without Water, this Day Master may be afflicted by loneliness, or be inclined towards leading a reclusive, hermit-like life. This is why Water must be at least present in the chart; otherwise, this Day Master would be hard-pressed to find support, especially when entering a Water Luck Period.

- Where Bing Fire penetrates to the Heavenly Stems, while Jia Wood or Ren Water is present, a thriving, favorable Fire Structure shall be formed. Should this Day Master enter Metal or Water Luck Period, however, he or she may be afflicted by serious setbacks and hardships in life. He or she will also be afflicted with loneliness.

- Where this Day Master encounters a Resource Structure, he or she shall at least be able to live an above-average life, with more than enough basic necessities to make life comfortable. Nevertheless, the circumstances in this Day Master's BaZi Chart would not augur well for his or her children.

Ding 丁 Fire Day Master, Born in Sixth Month 六月

Wei 未 (Goat) Month
July 7th - August 7th

Do note that the dates provided above are subject to slight yearly variations. Please refer to the Ten Thousand Year Calendar for the accurate transition dates for each year.

| Day Master | Ding 丁 Fire | Month | Wei 未 (Goat) |

Goat

日元 Day Master	月 Month
丁 Ding Yin Fire	未 Wei Goat Yin Earth

For a Ding Fire Day Master born in a Wei (Goat) Month, an Eating God Structure is formed where Ji Earth is revealed as one of the Heavenly Stems.

Where Yi Wood is revealed as one of the Heavenly Stems, an Indirect Resource Structure is formed.

Where Ding Fire is revealed as one of the Heavenly Stems, a Thriving Structure may be formed when the conditions are completely met and supported by the Earthly branches.

Should, however, neither Yi Wood, Ding Fire nor Ji Earth happen to be revealed within the Heavenly Stems, one should select the BaZi Chart's most prominent Qi attribute at one's discretion.

Day Master	Ding 丁 Fire		Month	Wei 未 (Goat)

喜用神提要 **Regulating Useful God Reference Guide**

月 **Month**	用神 **Useful God**
6th Month 六月 Wei 未 **(Goat) Month**	甲 壬 庚 *Jia* *Ren* *Geng* **Yang Wood** **Yang Water** **Yang Metal**

Goat

For a Wei (Goat) Month, Jia Wood, Ren Water and Geng Metal are the Regulating Useful Gods.

As a Useful God, Jia Wood comforts the Ren Water, whilst maintaining the shine of Ding Fire.

Jia Wood must, however, be used in tandem with Geng Metal – which plays the role of a supporting Useful God.

143

| Day Master | Ding 丁 Fire | Month | Wei 未 (Goat) |

7th day of July – 7th day of August, Gregorian Calendar

Although the Wei (Goat) Earthly Branch serves as storage for excess Wood Qi, Earth nonetheless features prominently at this particular time of the year.

Under such circumstances, Fire would tend to be more weakened than produced or strengthened in general. In other words, Fire Qi – no matter how hot or blazing – will be gradually reduced.

Wood, as a Resource Star, is hence still the primary Useful God, since it produces and strengthens Fire. Then and only then may Water be used to provide 'moisture' and reduce the 'dryness' of Earth.

Metal and Water – in moderate quantities – should therefore be 'added' to a Day Master born in an hour where Wood and Fire are strong, so that Ding Fire will not be 'extinguished'. Then and only then will this person prosper and become wealthy in life.

The presence or absence of Water also determines the luck of the husbands of female Day Masters. Where Metal is present in overabundance, however, it would 'hurt' and exert an overly strong control over Wood – which is Day Master's Useful God.

六月 Sixth Month

Goat

| Day Master | Ding 丁 Fire | Month | Wei 未 (Goat) |

Commentary

In addition to the preceding narratives on the potential Structures and scenarios resulting from a Ding Fire Day Master born in a Wei (Goat) Month, the following circumstances also play their respective roles in determining the overall strength of this Day Master's BaZi Chart.

Note:

- Of all the Five Elements, Jia Wood is the primary and most-preferred Useful God for this Ding Fire Day Master.

- Meanwhile, Ren Water serves as the Regulating Useful God to this Day Master.

- A best-case scenario for this Day Master would be where the Hai (Pig), Mao (Rabbit) and Wei (Goat) Earthly Branches form a full Wood Structure – and while Ren Water and Jia Wood are both revealed in the Heavenly Stems. Under such circumstances, this Day Master shall enjoy immense success and fulfillment in life.

- Where Jia Wood is revealed in the Heavenly Stems – while there is no Wood Structure formed in the Earthly Branches – this Day Master would only be able to lead an average life at best with lack of significant achievements, no matter how knowledgeable he or she may be; even with the presence of Ren Water.

- Where Jia Wood is revealed in the Heavenly Stems – but Geng Metal is missing – this Day Master may search in vain for a sense of peace throughout his or her entire life.

- Where the Earthly Branches form a full Wood Structure – but only Ren Water is revealed in the Heavenly Stems but Jia Wood is not – this Wood Structure would still be considered useless one. And under such circumstances, this person may have many goals and dreams, but no perseverance to see through his or her idea.

- Where the BaZi Chart consists of four Ding Fire-Wei (Goat) Pillars, the extremely Yin nature of the chart would probably bring about a Day Master who happens to be born into a large family. This Day Master may also find it difficult to establish his or her own career path, or carve his or her own niche in life. Nevertheless, the wives of such male Day Masters will tend to wield real authority in the household, and be able to even manage the affairs of others. It would hence be safe to say that this Day Master shall be blessed with good luck in life, although he will lack real power or authority.

Goat

六月 Sixth Month

🌱
Goat

| Day Master | Ding 丁 Fire | | Month | Wei 未 (Goat) |

Additional Attributes

格局 Structural Star	正印 Direct Resource	正官 Direct Officer
用神 Useful God	Jia 甲 Wood	Ren 壬 Water
Conditions	Where Geng Metal (Direct Wealth Star) is present, this Day Master shall enjoy prosperity and wealth in life.	
Positive Circumstances	Presence of Geng Metal.	
Negative Circumstances	Ji Earth intermingles with and 'contaminates' Ren Water (Direct Officer Star).	

* *Jia Wood and Ren Water are the preferred Useful Gods for a Ding Fire Day Master born in a Wei (Goat) Month.*

Day Master	Ding 丁 Fire		Month	Wei 未 (Goat)

Summary

- In the first-half of a Wei (Goat) Month, Ren Water (Direct Officer Star) serves as the primary Useful God to this Day Master.

- In the second-half of a Wei (Goat) Month, Jia Wood (Direct Resource Star) serves as this Day Master's primary Useful God.

- A BaZi Chart that is extremely Yin in nature may lack a sense of purpose and direction in life. No matter how large and powerful his or her family may be, this Day Master may still find it difficult to achieve any success in life.

- It would be best to avoid having two Bing Fire elements flanking Ding Fire. Otherwise, this Day Master may be afflicted by poverty in the early stages of his or her life. An in later stages, much of his or her success is overshadowed by his friends or siblings. Nevertheless, where Water is revealed, this situation may be averted.

六
月

Sixth Month

Goat

147

Ding 丁 Fire Day Master, Born in Seventh Month 七月

Shen 申 (Monkey) Month
August 8th - September 7th

Do note that the dates provided above are subject to slight yearly variations. Please refer to the Ten Thousand Year Calendar for the accurate transition dates for each year.

Day Master Ding 丁 Fire　　**Month** Shen 申 (Monkey)

日元 Day Master	月 Month
丁 Ding Yin Fire	申 Shen Monkey Yang Metal

For a Ji Earth Day Master born in a Shen (Monkey) Month, a Direct Wealth Structure is formed where Geng Metal is revealed as one of the Heavenly Stems.

Where Ren Water is revealed as one of the Heavenly Stems, a Direct Officer Structure is formed.

Where Wu Earth is revealed as one of the Heavenly Stems, a Hurting Officer Structure is formed.

Should, however, neither Geng Metal nor Ren Water nor Wu Earth happen to be revealed amongst the Heavenly Stems, one should select a Structure according to the BaZi Chart's most prominent Qi attribute at one's discretion.

| Day Master | Ding 丁 Fire | Month | Shen 申 (Monkey) |

喜用神提要 Regulating Useful God Reference Guide

月 Month	用神 Useful God
7th Month 七月 **Shen 申 (Monkey) Month**	甲 *Jia* **Yang Wood** 庚 *Geng* **Yang Metal** 丙 *Bing* **Yang Fire** 戊 *Wu* **Yang Earth**

Monkey

For a Shen (Monkey) Month, Jia Wood, Geng Meal, Bing Fire and Wu Earth are the Regulating Useful Gods.

Geng Metal is used to condition Jia Wood. In the absence of Jia Wood, Yi Wood may be employed in its stead.

Meanwhile, Bing Fire should be used to 'warm' Metal, as well as 'dry' Jia Wood.

Should neither Geng Metal nor Jia Wood happen to be present – and Yi Wood is used instead of Jia Wood – Yi Wood, which is akin to 'dry' grass, will serve to absorb the light brought about by Bing Fire.

Where Water is strong, Wu Earth may be used to keep it under control.

七月 Seventh Month

Monkey

Day Master	Ding 丁 Fire	Month	Shen 申 (Monkey)

8th day of August – 7th day of September, Gregorian Calendar

Geng Metal is at its strongest, in a Shen (Monkey) Month. Water Qi is also quite prominent in this Month.

Due to their individual and combined strength, Metal and Water have the capacity to weaken Ding Fire. And where Metal Qi is present in abundance, Wood – Resource Star – would also be 'hurt' and weakened. Water, when present in abundance, would also cause Wood to become 'damp' and 'wet'.

This is why both Wood and Fire are needed as Useful Gods, since their combined support will bring balance to this Day Master, and allow it to become a 'sentimental' one.

Where Ren Water penetrates to the Heavenly Stems in the case of female Day Masters – while Wood is also present in the Earthly Branches – the combination of Ding Fire and Ren Water would allow these Day Masters to enjoy excellent relationships with their husbands.

Day Master	Ding 丁 Fire		Month	Shen 申 (Monkey)

Commentary

In addition to the preceding narratives on the potential Structures and scenarios resulting from a Ding Fire Day Master born in a Shen (Monkey) Month, the following circumstances also play their respective roles in determining the overall strength of this Day Master's BaZi Chart.

Monkey

Note:

- The Regulating Useful Gods for a Ding Fire Day Master born in any of the autumn months of Shen (Monkey), You (Rooster) or Xu (Dog) are basically the same. The criteria for deciding the Useful Gods for a Day Master born in any of these three months are quite similar.

- Geng Metal is at its strongest in a Shen (Monkey) Month. Consequently, this would mean that Ren Water continues to be produced.

- Where Geng Metal (Direct Wealth) is too strong, it is likely that the wives of male Day Masters would be the ones wielding real authority and power.

- Where Ren Water is present in abundance and also penetrates to the Heavenly Stems – in the process combining with Ding Fire to form Wood – and under such circumstances, this Day Master can enjoy prosperity and become very wealthy in life.

- Where Geng Metal is present in abundance but Ren Water is missing, the former would invariably 'hurt' Jia Wood, which is this Day Master's Useful God. Under such circumstances, this Day Master may be afflicted by serious setbacks and possibly even poverty – to the extent of even becoming homeless – in life.

- In the absence of Jia Wood, Yi Wood and Bing Fire may be used simultaneously to substitute it. In any case, Jia Wood should never be parted from Geng Metal; while Yi Wood should never be parted from Bing Fire.

- If Yi Wood is used to account for the absence of Jia Wood, this Day Master may only lead a slightly above average life, at best.

153

Day Master	Ding 丁 Fire		Month	Shen 申 (Monkey)

Additional Attributes

格局 Structural Star	正印 Direct Resource	正財 Direct Wealth	劫財 Rob Wealth
用神 Useful God	Jia 甲 Wood	Geng 庚 Metal	Bing 丙 Fire
Conditions	This Day Master shall lead a life of superior quality, where Jia Wood, Geng Metal and Bing Fire are all revealed.		
Positive Circumstances	Bing Fire, Jia Wood and Geng Metal revealed in the Heavenly Stems.		
Negative Circumstances	Absence of Jia Wood in the chart.		

格局 Structural Star	正官 Direct Officer	七殺 Seven Killings
用神 Useful God	Ren 壬 Water	Gui 癸 Water
Conditions	Where Gui Water is present and rooted, Wu Earth (Hurting Officer Star) and Ji Earth (Eating God Star) should be used to keep Gui Water under control.	
Positive Circumstances	Jia Wood and Bing Fire must nonetheless be present in the chart.	
Negative Circumstances	Absence of Wu Earth and Ji Earth.	

Day Master	Ding 丁 Fire	Month	Shen 申 (Monkey)

Additional Attributes

格局 **Structural Star**	正財 Direct Wealth
用神 **Useful God**	Geng 庚 Metal
Conditions	A Follow the Wealth Structure may be formed if a full Metal Structure in the Branches are present and with total absent of wood and fire Qi.
Positive Circumstances	Ren Water present.
Negative Circumstances	Without Ren Water, this Day Master may drift and wander aimlessly in life. Absence of Fire and Wood should a Follow Wealth be formed.

Monkey

* *Jia Wood and Geng Metal are the preferred Useful Gods for a Ding Fire Day Master born in a Shen (Monkey) Month.*

155

BaZi Structures & Structural Useful Gods 格局與格局用神

Day Master Ding 丁 Fire	**Month** Shen 申 (Monkey)

Summary

七月 Seventh Month

Monkey

- Where a Follow the Wealth Structure is formed, it should not be weakened or clashed with. Otherwise, its presence and usefulness would be negated and instead of prosperity, disaster would follow.

- Bing Fire provides 'warmth' and hence supports this Day Master in this month. However, it would be preferable for Bing Fire not to be present in the Stems but rather, in the Earthly Branches.

Ding 丁 Fire Day Master, Born in Eighth Month 八月

You 酉 (Rooster) Month
September 8th - October 7th

Do note that the dates provided above are subject to slight yearly variations. Please refer to the Ten Thousand Year Calendar for the accurate transition dates for each year.

八月

Eighth Month

Rooster

| Day Master | Ding 丁 Fire | Month | You 酉 (Rooster) |

日元 Day Master	月 Month
丁 *Ding* **Yin Fire**	酉 *You* **Rooster** **Yin Metal**

For a Ding Fire Day Master born in a You (Rooster) Month, an Indirect Wealth Structure is formed where Xin Metal is revealed as one of the Heavenly Stems.

Even if Ding Fire is not revealed as a Heavenly Stem, an Indirect Wealth Structure would still be considered to have been formed.

| Day Master | Ding 丁 Fire | Month | You 酉 (Rooster) |

喜用神提要 Regulating Useful God Reference Guide

Rooster

月 Month	用神 Useful God
8th Month 八月 **You 酉 (Rooster) Month**	甲 *Jia* **Yang Wood** 庚 *Geng* **Yang Metal** 丙 *Bing* **Yang Fire** 戊 *Wu* **Yang Earth**

For a You (Rooster) Month, Jia Wood, Geng Metal, Bing Fire and Wu Earth are the Regulating Useful Gods.

Geng Metal is used to 'condition' and keep Jia Wood under control. In the absence of Jia Wood, Yi Wood may be used in its stead.

Should neither Geng Metal nor Jia Wood be present – and Yi Wood is used instead of Jia Wood – Yi Wood, which is akin to 'dry' grass, will serve to absorb the light brought about by Bing Fire.

Where Water is strong, Wu Earth may be used to keep it under control.

八月

Eighth Month

酉
Rooster

Day Master Ding 丁 Fire	Month You 酉 (Rooster)

8th day of September – 7th day of October, Gregorian Calendar

Metal is at its strongest in this month. The Yin Metal nature of the You (Rooster) Earthly Branch would also clash with the roots of Wood, which is one of this Day Master's Useful Gods.

Thus, it is inferred that the strength and Qi of Wood – the Resource Star – would be extremely limited. And without Wood, it would be difficult for Ding Fire to 'shine' and 'sparkle'.

As such, Wood and Fire are the most important Useful Gods for this Day Master.

The strong presence of Metal and Water Qi would, however, weaken Fire most, of all the Five Elements.

In addition, there is also the need to avoid having 'wet' or 'moist' Earth produce Metal, which is already strong. This is because where Metal – the Wealth Star – is present in abundance; this Day Master would be severely weakened.

The company of Friend Stars would also greatly assist this Day Master, especially in helping him or her to prosper in life.

Where this Day Master enters a Metal or Water Luck Period – without the assistance of Wood as a Useful God – he or she may be plagued by legal issues and lawsuits, throughout his or her life.

Day Master	Ding 丁 Fire		Month	You 酉 (Rooster)

Commentary

In addition to the preceding narratives on the potential Structures and scenarios resulting from a Ding Fire Day Master born in a You (Rooster) Month, the following circumstances also play their respective roles in determining the overall strength of this Day Master's BaZi Chart.

Note:

- The Regulating Useful Gods for a Ding Fire Day Master born in any of the autumn months of Shen (Monkey), You (Rooster) or Xu (Dog) are basically the same. The criteria for deciding the Useful Gods for a Day Master born in any of these three months are almost similar.

- Where only Xin Metal is revealed but Friend and Rob Wealth Stars are missing, it would be possible for a Follow the Wealth Structure to be formed. Nevertheless, Geng Metal must not be revealed in the Heavenly Stems as well.

Rooster

八
月

Eighth Month

161

BaZi Structures & Structural Useful Gods 格局與格局用神

| **Day Master** Ding 丁 Fire | **Month** You 酉 (Rooster) |

Additional Attributes

格局 **Structural Star**	偏財 Indirect Wealth
用神 **Useful God**	Xin 辛 Metal
Conditions	Where only Xin Metal (Indirect Wealth Star) is revealed but Geng Metal (Direct Wealth Star) is not, it would be possible to have a Follow the Wealth Structure formed in the BaZi Chart. Where this structure is successfully formed, a life of great achievements awaits. Eventhough there will be many challenges, but each event leads to an even greater achievement
Positive Circumstances	Absence of additional Fire or Wood Element.
Negative Circumstances	Friend, Rob Wealth and Resource Stars are present.

* Xin Metal, Jia Wood and Bing Fire are the preferred Useful Gods for a Ding Fire Day Master born in a You (Rooster) Month.

Eighth Month — Rooster 酉

| Day Master | Ding 丁 Fire | Month | You 酉 (Rooster) |

Summary

- When this Day Master is not directly entering a Follow the Wealth Structure – but instead displays an affinity with Xin Metal (Indirect Wealth Star) – Friend and Rob Wealth Stars should not be encountered.

- In ordinary circumstances, Bing Fire and Jia Wood must not be missing from the BaZi Chart.

- Wealth Stars are preferred to Officer Stars, as Useful Gods for this Day Master.

- Where Gui Water (Seven Killings Star) is present, Wu Earth and Ji Earth are also required to keep Gui Water under control.

- Where Ren Water (Direct Officer Star) is present, it would not be preferable to have Ren Water combine with Ding Fire.

八月

Eighth Month

Rooster

163

Ding 丁 Fire Day Master, Born in Ninth Month 九月

Xu 戌 (Dog) Month
October 8th - November 6th

Do note that the dates provided above are subject to slight yearly variations. Please refer to the Ten Thousand Year Calendar for the accurate transition dates for each year.

BaZi Structures & Structural Useful Gods 格局與格局用神

| Day Master | Ding 丁 Fire | Month | Xu 戌 (Dog) |

日元 Day Master	月 Month
丁 Ding Yin Fire	戌 Xu Dog Yang Earth

For a Ding Fire Day Master born in a Xu (Dog) Month, a Hurting Officer Structure is formed where Wu Earth is revealed as one of the Heavenly Stems.

Where Xin Metal is revealed as one of the Heavenly Stems, an Indirect Wealth Structure is formed.

Where Ding Fire is revealed as one of the Heavenly Stems, a Thriving Structure may be formed when the conditions are completely met and supported by the Earthly branches.

Should, however, neither Wu Earth nor Xin Metal happen to be revealed amongst the Heavenly Stems, one should select a Structure according to the BaZi Chart's most prominent Qi attribute at one's discretion.

| Day Master | Ding 丁 Fire | | Month | Xu 戌 (Dog) |

喜用神提要 **Regulating Useful God Reference Guide**

月 **Month**	用神 **Useful God**		
9th Month 九月 **Xu** 戌 **(Dog) Month**	甲 *Jia* **Yang Wood**	庚 *Geng* **Yang Metal**	戊 *Wu* **Yang Earth**

Dog

For a Xu (Dog) Month, Jia Wood, Geng Metal and Wu Earth are the Regulating Useful Gods.

Where only Wu Earth is available as a Useful God and Jia Wood is not, Wu Earth (Hurting Officer Star) would be adversely affected.

九月 **Ninth Month**

Dog 戌

| Day Master | Ding 丁 Fire | Month | Xu 戌 (Dog) |

8th day of October – 6th day of November, Gregorian Calendar

In a Xu (Dog) Month, Earth is 'thick' and 'leaden', while Fire is also in storage.

As such, Wood should not be missing as a Useful God. This chart faces the risk of becoming overly 'dry' and 'parched'. This is why Wood serves as the primary Useful God, with Water as its secondary Useful God.

Meanwhile, Wood may also be used to 'loosen' Wu Earth. Likewise, Wood may also be used to produce and strengthen Ding Fire. Only then will the 'dry', 'scorched' Earth be able to be 'moistened' and serve as this Day Master's Useful God.

A Day Master born in an hour when Fire and Earth happen to be strong may also use Geng Metal to prevent Earth - which is 'thick' and 'leaden' – from 'breaking' Wood.

Day Master	Ding 丁 Fire	Month	Xu 戌 (Dog)

Commentary

In addition to the preceding narratives on the potential Structures and scenarios resulting from a Ding Fire Day Master born in a Xu (Dog) Month, the following circumstances also play their respective roles in determining the overall strength of this Day Master's BaZi Chart.

Note:

- The Regulating Useful Gods for a Ding Fire Day Master born in any of the autumn months of Shen (Monkey), You (Rooster) or Xu (Dog) are basically the same. Indeed, the criteria for deciding the Useful Gods for a Day Master born in any of these three months are almost similar.

- Where only Wood Structures are formed in the BaZi Chart – while Ren Water and Jia Wood remain missing – Wu Earth, this Day Master's Hurting Officer Star, would be the adversely affected. Nevertheless, this Day Master shall still be blessed with fame, authority and power in life despite discontentment.

- Without Jia Wood as a Useful God, this Day Master would still be a learned, knowledgeable one, but the level of success is merely ordinary.

九月 Ninth Month

Dog

169

Day Master	Ding 丁 Fire	Month	Xu 戌 (Dog)

Additional Attributes

格局 Structural Star	傷官 Hurting Officer	偏財 Indirect Wealth	比肩 Friend
用神 **Useful God**	Wu 戊 Earth	Xin 辛 Metal	Ding 丁 Fire

Conditions	Where Wu Earth, Xin Metal and Ding Fire all occupy the same Palace and are also revealed in the Heavenly Stems, a situation known as Ti Yong Tong Gong 體用同宮 (Bodies Occupying the Same Palace) occurs. And without Ren Water and Jia Wood to penetrate to the Heavenly Stems, this Day Master shall prosper in life.
Positive Circumstances	Any of the 3 hidden stems found in the Month Branch appearing in the Heavenly Stems.
Negative Circumstances	Ren Water and Jia Wood penetrate to the Heavenly Stems.

| Day Master | Ding 丁 Fire | | Month | Xu 戌 (Dog) |

Additional Attributes

格局 **Structural Star**	傷官 Hurting Officer
用神 **Useful God**	Wu 戊 Earth
Conditions	Where only Wu Earth (Hurting Officer Star) is available as a Useful God, Ren Water and Jia Wood should not be seen.
Positive Circumstances	Where Jia Wood is present, it must be accompanied by Geng Metal.
Negative Circumstances	The presence of Ren Water and Jia Wood, which adversely affect Wu Earth (Hurting Officer Star).

戌
Dog

* *Jia Wood and Geng Metal are the preferred Useful Gods for a Ding Fire Day Master born in a Xu (Dog) Month.*

九
月

Ninth Month

| Day Master | Ding 丁 Fire | Month | Xu 戌 (Dog) |

Summary

- A Hurting Officer Structure is the most-preferred Structure to have formed in the BaZi Chart of this Day Master.

- Where a Hurting Officer Structure is formed, Ren Water (Direct Officer Star) should be avoided or at least, not be encountered during the cycles.

- Where the Chen (Dragon), Xu (Dog), Chou (Ox) and Wei (Goat) Earthly Branches are all present – while neither Ren Water nor Jia Wood penetrates to the Heavenly Stems – this Day Master shall enjoy prosperity in life.

- Where a Hurting Officer Structure is formed and Jia Wood revealed, Wu Earth (as the Hurting Officer Star) would be deemed to have 'utilized' and hence 'drained' Jia Wood (Direct Resource Star) of its strength. Nonetheless, under such circumstances, this Day Master would still be a learned, knowledgeable one albeit lack of wealth and achievements.

戌
Dog

Ding 丁 Fire Day Master, Born in Tenth Month 十月

Hai 亥 (Pig) Month
November 7th - December 6th

Do note that the dates provided above are subject to slight yearly variations. Please refer to the Ten Thousand Year Calendar for the accurate transition dates for each year.

十月 Tenth Month

亥 Pig

| Day Master | Ding 丁 Fire | Month | Hai 亥 (Pig) |

日元 Day Master	月 Month
丁 Ding Yin Fire	亥 Hai Pig Yin Water

For a Ding Fire Day Master born in a Pig (Hai) Month, a Direct Officer Structure is formed where Ren Water is revealed as one of the Heavenly Stems.

Where Jia Wood is revealed as one of the Heavenly Stems, a Direct Resource Structure is formed.

Should, however, neither Ren Water nor Jia Wood happen to be revealed amongst the Heavenly Stems, one should select a Structure according to the BaZi Chart's most prominent Qi attribute at one's discretion.

| Day Master | Ding 丁 Fire | Month | Hai 亥 (Pig) |

喜用神提要 Regulating Useful God Reference Guide

月 Month	用神 Useful God
10th Month 十月 Hai 亥 (Pig) Month	**甲** *Jia* **Yang Wood** **庚** *Geng* **Yang Metal**

Pig

For a Hai (Pig) Month, Jia Wood and Geng Metal are the Regulating Useful Gods.

Geng Metal is used to chop Jia Wood, as well as 'attract' Ding Fire.

Jia Wood is the primary Useful God to this Day Master, while Geng Metal is its secondary Useful God.

Where either is not available, Wu Earth and Gui Water may also be employed as substitute Useful Gods.

| Day Master Ding 丁 Fire | Month Hai 亥 (Pig) |

7th day of November – 6th day of December, Gregorian Calendar

Water is dominant in a Hai (Pig) Month.

Given the early winter timing of this Day Master's birth, his or her BaZi Chart's Qi would invariably tend to be cold, with Wood 'moist' and 'wet'. And although the Hai (Pig) Earthly Branch contains Jia Wood as one of its Hidden Stems, it would still be impossible for 'wet' Wood to produce Fire.

Fire is one of the most important Useful Gods for this Day Master. This Day Master will only truly excel, where Wood and Fire are both present, and are used together with the Ren Water Hidden Stem contained within the Hai (Pig) Earthly Branch.

Female Ding Fire Day Masters with Wood and Fire in their Day and Hour Pillars would, however, find it easy to attract and marry wealthy husbands, where Ren Water is seen penetrating to the Heavenly Stems.

Pig

Day Master	Ding 丁 Fire	Month	Hai 亥 (Pig)

十
月

Tenth Month

Commentary

In addition to the preceding narratives on the potential Structures and scenarios resulting from a Ding Fire Day Master born in a Hai (Pig) Month, the following circumstances also play their respective roles in determining the overall strength of this Day Master's BaZi Chart.

Pig

Note:

- Where Jia Wood (Direct Resource Star) is present and penetrates to the Heavenly Stems, a Ding Fire Day Master born in a the Hai (Pig), Zi (Rat) or Chou (Ox) Month - shall at least, be able to lead a life of quality and comfort.

- Jia Wood serves as the primary Regulating Useful God for a Day Master born in either a Hai (Pig), Zi (Rat) or Chou (Ox) Month,

- Bing Fire should also be present as yet another important Useful God. Since Fire is the Self Element of a Ding Fire Day Master, however, there would be no need for Bing Fire to penetrate to the Heavenly Stems. In fact, it would be preferable to avoid having Bing Fire present in abundance in the Heavenly Stems.

- Where at least one Bing Fire element is seen in the Heavenly Stems, Metal and Water would be needed to keep Bing Fire under control.

- Where Bing Fire 'steals' or 'snatches' the 'shine' or 'luster' of its Ding Fire counterpart, this Day Master may lack a sense of purpose and direction in life, more so where additional Metal and Water Qi are missing from the BaZi Chart.

- Where Metal is present but additional Water stars are missing, this Day Master may still be afflicted by poverty in life; no matter how learned or knowledgeable he or she may be.

- Where Ren Water is present but Metal missing, this Day Master may lack actual power or authority; regardless of his or her status or academic achievements in life.

- Where two Ren Water elements are present in the Month and Hour Pillars, and compete with one another to combine with Ding Fire, Wu Earth may be used to neutralize Ren Water. Even with Wu Earth present under such circumstances, this Day Master may only be able to lead an average life, at best.

- Where Wu Earth does not penetrate to the Heavenly Stems, this Day Master may only possess a mediocre, average capacity to succeed in life.

- Where Wu Earth remains as one of the Hidden Stems of the Earthly Branches, this Day Master may also only be able to lead an average life, at best.

- Where two Bing Fire elements attempt to 'snatch' or 'steal' the 'luster' and 'shine' of Ding Fire, this Day Master would still be able to enjoy power and authority in life albeit one that is not so contented; even without Gui Water present as an intermediary Useful God.

- Where Resource and Friend Stars are missing – with Metal and Water present in abundance – resulting in a possible Follow the Killings Structure being formed, this Day Master shall enjoy a high level of authority and status in life. If this special formation is successful, an extraordinary life awaits.

- Jia Wood is the primary Useful God to a Ding Fire Day Master born in a winter month. It must, however, be employed together with Geng Metal, since both serve as the most important Useful Gods to this Day Master.

BaZi Structures & Structural Useful Gods 格局與格局用神

Day Master Ding 丁 Fire		Month Hai 亥 (Pig)
Additional Attributes		

格局 Structural Star	正印 Direct Resource	正財 Direct Wealth
用神 Useful God	Jia 甲 Wood	Geng 庚 Metal
Conditions	Jia Wood (Direct Resource Star) is the primary Useful God for this Day Master. With its presence, this Day Master shall at least be able to enjoy success in his or her career-related pursuits.	
Positive Circumstances	Jia Wood penetrated to the Heavenly Stems.	
Negative Circumstances	Ji Earth (Eating God Star) penetrates to the Heavenly Stems and combines Jia Wood away, to form Earth.	

格局 Structural Star	正官 Direct Officer
用神 Useful God	Ren 壬 Water
Conditions	As a Direct Officer Star, it would nonetheless be unfavourable for two Ren Water elements to simultaneously penetrate to the Heavenly Stems. This is because both Direct Officer Stars will compete with one another to combine with Ding Fire. And if this is the case, this Day Master would lead a confusing life, a life that seem to be laden with many difficult crossroads and dicey relationships.
Positive Circumstances	The presence of Wu Earth (Hurting Officer Star), to neutralize at least one Ren Water element.
Negative Circumstances	Two Ren Water flanking the Day Master.

| Day Master | Ding 丁 Fire | | Month | Hai 亥 (Pig) |

Additional Attributes

Pig

格局 Structural Star	劫財 Rob Wealth
用神 Useful God	Bing 丙 Fire
Conditions	Where one Bing Fire element penetrates to the Heavenly Stems, this Day Master would only lead an average life, at best. Where two Bing Fire elements penetrate to the Heavenly Stems – accompanied by one Gui Water element - this Day Master has the potential to become really famous in life.
Positive Circumstances	Bing Fire meeting Gui Water.
Negative Circumstances	Absence of Gui Water.

格局 Structural Star	正印 Direct Resource	偏財 Indirect Wealth
用神 Useful God	Jia 甲 Wood	Yi 乙 Wood
Conditions	Where the Hai (Pig), Mao (Rabbit) and Wei (Goat) Earthly Branches are all present in the BaZi Chart, this Day Master may still succeed in life; although much of his or her success would be due to the support and assistance of others.	
Positive Circumstances	Jia Wood penetrating to the Heavenly Stems.	
Negative Circumstances	Neither Jia nor Yi Wood penetrating to the Heavenly Stems.	

*   *Jia Wood and Geng Metal are the preferred Useful Gods for a Ding Fire Day Master born in a Hai (Pig) Month.*

** *The Useful Gods for a Day Master born in either a Hai (Pig), Zi (Rat) or Chou (Ox) Month are basically the same.*

179

BaZi Structures & Structural Useful Gods 格局與格局用神

| Day Master | Ding 丁 Fire | Month | Hai 亥 (Pig) |

Summary

- The Useful Gods and general theories regarding a Ding Fire Day Master born in any of the Hai (Pig), Zi (Rat) or Chou (Ox) winter months are basically the same.

- Jia Wood (Direct Resource Star) must also be accompanied by Geng Metal (Direct Wealth Star), as both are equally important as Useful Gods.

- It would be futile even attempting to substitute Jia Wood and Geng Metal with Yi Wood and Xin Metal respectively, since the latter two elements would be of no use as Useful Gods.

Ding 丁 Fire Day Master, Born in Eleventh Month 十一月

Zi 子 (Rat) Month
December 7th - January 5th

Do note that the dates provided above are subject to slight yearly variations. Please refer to the Ten Thousand Year Calendar for the accurate transition dates for each year.

十一月 Eleventh Month

Rat

| Day Master | Ding 丁 Fire | Month | Zi 子 (Rat) |

日元 Day Master	月 Month
丁	子
Ding	*Zi*
Yin Fire	**Rat**
	Yang Water

For a Ding Fire Day Master born in a Zi (Rat) Month, a Seven Killings Structure is formed where Gui Water is revealed as one of the Heavenly Stems.

Even if Gui Water is not revealed as a Heavenly Stem, a Seven Killings Structure would still be considered to have been formed.

Day Master	Ding 丁 Fire		Month	Zi 子 (Rat)

喜用神提要 Regulating Useful God Reference Guide

月 Month	用神 Useful God
11th Month 十一月 Zi 子 (Rat) Month	甲 *Jia* **Yang Wood** 庚 *Geng* **Yang Metal**

Rat

For a Zi (Rat) Month, Jia Wood and Geng Metal are the Regulating Useful Gods.

Geng Metal is used to 'split or chop' Jia Wood, as well as 'attract' Ding Fire.

Jia Wood is the primary Useful God to this Day Master, with Geng Metal as its secondary Useful God.

Where either is not available, Wu Earth and Gui Water may also be employed as substitute Useful Gods.

十一月 Eleventh Month

BaZi Structures & Structural Useful Gods 格局與格局用神

| Day Master | Ding 丁 Fire | Month | Zi 子 (Rat) |

7th day of December – 5th day of January, Gregorian Calendar

Water is inevitably cold and possibly frozen into ice, in a Zi (Rat) Month. Under such circumstances, Ding Fire is 'isolated', without any help present within the immediate vicinity.

This is why 'hot' or 'blazing' Wood harboring Fire Qi is needed, to counter and weaken Water, at least to an acceptable extent. Such Wood will also produce and ensure the continuity of Fire.

Needless to say, without Wood and Fire being rooted in their respective elements, it would be rather impossible for Ding Fire to continue 'burning' or 'sparkling' at this time of the year by itself.

One should therefore note that in a Zi (Rat) Month, Water is at its peak or strongest, and will more likely than not 'hurt' and weaken Fire Qi.

Metal, meanwhile, counters and weakens Wood; while Water exerts an overly strong control over Fire. As such, it would be undesirable for this Day Master to go through Metal and Wood Qi Luck Cycles.

Day Master	Ding 丁 Fire	Month	Zi 子 (Rat)

Commentary

In addition to the preceding narratives on the potential Structures and scenarios resulting from a Ding Fire Day Master born in a Zi (Rat) Month, the following circumstances also play their respective roles in determining the overall strength of this Day Master's BaZi Chart.

Note:

- Where Jia Wood – Direct Resource Star – is present and penetrates to the Heavenly Stems, a Ding Fire Day Master born in a winter month (i.e. Hai (Pig), Zi (Rat) or Chou (Ox) shall be able to, at minimum, lead a life of quality and comfort. Without Jia Wood, any structure would merely be a substandard one.

- Jia Wood serves as the primary Regulating Useful God for a Day Master born in either a Hai (Pig), Zi (Rat) or Chou (Ox) Month.

- Bing Fire should also be present, as yet another important Useful God. Since Fire is the Self Element of a Ding Fire Day Master, however, there would be no need for Bing Fire to penetrate to the Heavenly Stems. In fact, it would be preferable to avoid having Bing Fire present in abundance in the Heavenly Stems.

- Where at least one Bing Fire element is seen in the Heavenly Stems, Metal and Water stars would be needed to 'split' and hence keep Bing Fire under control.

- Where Bing Fire 'steals' or 'snatches' the 'shine' or 'luster' of its Ding Fire counterpart, this Day Master may lack a sense of purpose and direction in life, more so where Metal and additional Water stars totally are missing from the BaZi Chart.

- Where Metal is present but additional Water stars are missing, this Day Master may still be afflicted by poverty in life; no matter how learned or knowledgeable he or she may be.

- Where Ren Water is present but Metal missing, this Day Master may lack actual power or authority; regardless of his or her status in life.

- Where two Ren Water elements are present in the Month and Hour Pillars, and compete with one another to combine with Ding Fire, Wu Earth may be used to neutralize Ren Water. Even with Wu Earth present under such circumstances, this Day Master may only be able to lead an average life, at best.

- Where Wu Earth does not penetrate to the Heavenly Stems, this Day Master may only possess a mediocre, average capacity to succeed in life.

- Where Wu Earth remains as one of the Hidden Stems of the Earthly Branches, this Day Master may also only be able to lead an average life, at best.

- Jia Wood is the primary Useful God to a Ding Fire Day Master born in a winter month. It must, however, be employed together with Geng Metal. Without Geng Metal, the Jia Wood cannot produce Ding Fire.

BaZi Structures & Structural Useful Gods 格局與格局用神

Day Master Ding 丁 Fire		**Month** Zi 子 (Rat)

Additional Attributes

格局 **Structural Star**	正印 Direct Resource	正財 Direct Wealth
用神 **Useful God**	Jia 甲 Wood	Geng 庚 Metal
Conditions	Jia Wood (Direct Resource Star) is the primary Useful God for this Day Master. With its presence, this Day Master shall at least be able to enjoy success in his or her career-related pursuits.	
Positive Circumstances	Jia Wood Penetrating to the Heavenly Stems. Presence of Geng Metal in the chart.	
Negative Circumstances	Ji Earth (Eating God Star) penetrates to the Heavenly Stems and combines Jia Wood away, to form Earth.	

格局 **Structural Star**	正官 Direct Officer
用神 **Useful God**	Ren 壬 Water
Conditions	As a Direct Officer Star, it would nonetheless be unfavourable for two Ren Water elements to simultaneously penetrate to the Heavenly Stems. This is because both Direct Officer Stars will compete with one another to combine with Ding Fire. And if this is the case, this Day Master would only be able to lead an average life, at best.
Positive Circumstances	The presence of Wu Earth (Hurting Officer Star), to neutralize at least one Ren Water element.
Negative Circumstances	Absence of Wu Earth in the chart.

| Day Master | Ding 丁 Fire | Month | Zi 子 (Rat) |

Additional Attributes

Rat

格局 Structural Star	劫財 Rob Wealth
用神 Useful God	Bing 丙 Fire
Conditions	Where one Bing Fire element penetrates to the Heavenly Stems, this Day Master would only lead an average life, at best. Where two Bing Fire elements penetrate to the Heavenly Stems – accompanied by one Gui Water element - this Day Master shall become famous in life.
Positive Circumstances	Bing Fire and Gui Water appearing simultaneously.
Negative Circumstances	Absence of Gui Water.

格局 Structural Star	正印 Direct Resource	偏財 Indirect Wealth
用神 Useful God	Jia 甲 Wood	Yi 乙 Wood
Conditions	Where the Hai (Pig), Mao (Rabbit) and Wei (Goat) Earthly Branches are all present in the BaZi Chart, this Day Master may still succeed in life; although much of his or her success would be due to the support and assistance of others.	
Positive Circumstances	Jia Wood or Yi Wood penetrating to the Heavenly Stems	
Negative Circumstances	Absence of Wood in the Heavenly Stems	

*   *Jia Wood and Geng Metal are the preferred Useful Gods for a Ding Fire Day Master born in a Zi (Rat) Month.*

** *The Useful Gods for a Day Master born in either a Hai (Pig), Zi (Rat) or Chou (Ox) Month are basically the same.*

187

十一月 Eleventh Month

Rat

| Day Master | Ding 丁 Fire | Month | Zi 子 (Rat) |

Summary

- The Useful Gods and general theories regarding a Ding Fire Day Master born in any of the winter months of Hai (Pig), Zi (Rat) or Chou (Ox) are basically the same.

- Nevertheless, Jia Wood (Direct Resource Star) must also be accompanied by Geng Metal (Direct Wealth Star), as both are equally important as Useful Gods.

- It would be futile even attempting to substitute Jia Wood and Geng Metal with Yi Wood and Xin Metal respectively, since the latter two elements would be of no use as Useful Gods.

Ding 丁 Fire Day Master, Born in Twelfth Month 十二月

Chou 丑 (Ox) Month
January 6th - February 3rd

Do note that the dates provided above are subject to slight yearly variations. Please refer to the Ten Thousand Year Calendar for the accurate transition dates for each year.

BaZi Structures & Structural Useful Gods 格局與格局用神

Day Master Ding 丁 Fire	Month Chou 丑 (Ox)

日元 **Day Master**	月 **Month**
丁 *Ding* **Yin Fire**	丑 *Chou* **Ox** **Yin Earth**

For a Ding Fire Day Master born in a Chou (Ox) Month, an Eating God Structure is formed where Ji Earth is revealed as one of the Heavenly Stems.

Where Xin Metal is revealed as one of the Heavenly Stems, an Indirect Wealth Structure is formed.

Where Gui Water is revealed as one of the Heavenly Stems, a Seven Killings Structure is formed.

Should, however, neither Ji Earth nor Gui Water nor Xin Metal happen to be revealed amongst the Heavenly Stems, one should select a Structure according to the BaZi Chart's most prominent Qi attribute at one's discretion.

| Day Master | Ding 丁 Fire | Month | Chou 丑 (Ox) |

喜用神提要 **Regulating Useful God Reference Guide**

Ox

月 **Month**	用神 **Useful God**
12th Month 十二月 Chou 丑 (Ox) **Month**	甲 *Jia* **Yang Wood** 庚 *Geng* **Yang Metal**

For a Chou (Ox) Month, Jia Wood and Geng Metal are the Regulating Useful Gods.

Geng Metal is used to 'split' Jia Wood, as well as 'attract' Ding Fire.

This would then allow Jia Wood to serve as the primary Useful God to this Day Master, with Geng Metal as the secondary Useful God.

Where either is not available, Wu Earth and Gui Water may also be employed as substitute Useful Gods.

191

BaZi Structures & Structural Useful Gods 格局與格局用神

Day Master Ding 丁 Fire	**Month** Chou 丑 (Ox)

6th day of January – 3rd day of February, Gregorian Calendar

Water, being very strong in a Chou (Ox) Month, would only produce 'wet' Earth. Metal Qi adds to the coldness of the environment. And this in turn, would only serve to further weaken this Ding Fire Day Master.

Even with Earth present, its frozen or overly cold Qi would not allow it to produce Wood at this time of the year. As a result, Wood – the Resource Star – would invariably be 'wet' and also dormant.

This is why Fire is needed to keep Metal under control and bring warmth. Meanwhile, Wood may be used to produce Fire, which in turn, shall strengthen this Day Master.

Wood should, however, carry or at least harbor some Fire Qi - as well as be rooted in its element - in order to serve as a Useful God to this Day Master.

It is only with the combined strength of Wood and Fire Qi that this Day Master may be duly strengthened and kept well-balanced. Furthermore, there is also the need for this Day Master to avoid further meeting Metal and Water Qi, as much as possible.

This is because Metal and Water have the capacity to counter and weaken Fire, as well as Wood. And such circumstances may affect this Day Master's wealth luck and health prospects in life.

十二月 Twelfth Month

Ox

| Day Master | Ding 丁 Fire | Month | Chou 丑 (Ox) |

Commentary

In addition to the preceding narratives on the potential Structures and scenarios resulting from a Ding Fire Day Master born in a Chou (Ox) Month, the following circumstances also play their respective roles in determining the overall strength of this Day Master's BaZi Chart.

Note:

- Where Jia Wood – Direct Resource Star – is present and penetrates to the Heavenly Stems, a Ding Fire Day Master born in a winter month (i.e. Hai (Pig), Zi (Rat) or Chou (Ox) shall, at minimum, be able to lead a life of good quality and superior comfort.

- Jia Wood serves as the Primary Regulating Useful Gods for a Day Master born in either a Hai (Pig), Zi (Rat) or Chou (Ox) Month.

- Bing Fire should also be present, as yet another important Useful God. Since Fire is the Self Element of a Ding Fire Day Master, however, there would be no need for Bing Fire to penetrate to the Heavenly Stems. In fact, it would be preferable to avoid having Bing Fire present in abundance in the Heavenly Stems. Bing Fire as the main Qi of the Earthly Branches would be sufficient.

- Where at least one Bing Fire element is seen in the Heavenly Stems, Metal and Water would be needed to keep Bing Fire under control.

- Where excessive, exposed Bing Fire 'steals' or 'snatches' the 'shine' or 'luster' of its Ding Fire counterpart, this Day Master may lack a sense of purpose and direction in life. He or she will feel that his or her achievements are overshadowed by friends or siblings.

- Where Metal is present but additional Water star is missing, this Day Master may still be afflicted by poverty and depression in life; no matter how learned or knowledgeable he or she may be.

- Where Ren Water is present but Metal star is missing, this Day Master may lack actual power or authority; regardless of his or her status or academic level in life.

- Where two Ren Water stars are present in the Month and Hour Pillars, and compete with one another to combine with Ding Fire, Wu Earth may be used to neutralize Ren Water. Even with Wu Earth present under such circumstances, this Day Master may only be able to lead an average life, at best.

- Where Wu Earth does not penetrate to the Heavenly Stems, this Day Master may only possess a mediocre, average capacity to succeed in life. There will always be feelings of discontentment and uncertainty throughout life.

- Where Wu Earth remains as one of the Hidden Stems of the Earthly Branches, this Day Master may also only be able to lead an average life, at best. Without Wu Earth, this person will not be able to excel and will lead a life full of self doubt or self sabotage.

- Where Resource and Friend Stars are missing – with Metal and Water Qi present in abundance – resulting in a possible Follow the Killings Structure being formed, this Day Master shall enjoy a high level of authority and status in life.

- Jia Wood is the primary Useful God to a Ding Fire Day Master born in a winter month. It must, however, be employed together with Geng Metal, since both serve as the most important Useful Gods to this Day Master.

Ox

Day Master Ding 丁 Fire		Month Chou 丑 (Ox)
Additional Attributes		

格局 Structural Star	正印 Direct Resource	正財 Direct Wealth
用神 Useful God	Jia 甲 Wood	Geng 庚 Metal
Conditions	Jia Wood (Direct Resource Star) is the primary Useful God for this Day Master. With its presence, this Day Master shall at least be able to enjoy high levels of success in his or her career-related pursuits.	
Positive Circumstances	Jia Wood penetrated to the Heavenly Stems.	
Negative Circumstances	Ji Earth (Eating God Star) penetrates to the Heavenly Stems and combines Jia Wood away, to form Earth.	

格局 Structural Star	正官 Direct Officer
用神 Useful God	Ren 壬 Water
Conditions	It would be unfavourable for two Ren Water elements to simultaneously penetrate to the Heavenly Stems. This is because both Direct Officer Stars will compete with one another to combine with Ding Fire. When this happens, the person leads a life lack of sense of purpose and direction. Constantly trapped in difficult and dicey situations.
Positive Circumstances	The presence of Wu Earth (Hurting Officer Star), to neutralize at least one Ren Water element.
Negative Circumstances	Two Ren Water flanking the Day Master.

Day Master	Ding 丁 Fire	**Month**	Chou 丑 (Ox)

Additional Attributes

Ox

格局 **Structural Star**	劫財 Rob Wealth
用神 **Useful God**	Bing 丙 Fire
Conditions	Where one Bing Fire element penetrates to the Heavenly Stems, this Day Master would only lead an average life, at best. Where two Bing Fire elements penetrate to the Heavenly Stems – accompanied by one Gui Water element - this Day Master may, in some strange twist of fate, become famous in life.
Positive Circumstances	Two Bing Fire. With one Gui Water.
Negative Circumstances	Absence of Gui Water.

格局 **Structural Star**	正印 Direct Resource	偏印 Indirect Resource
用神 **Useful God**	Jia 甲 Wood	Yi 乙 Wood
Conditions	Where the Hai (Pig), Mao (Rabbit) and Wei (Goat) Earthly Branches are all present in the BaZi Chart, this Day Master may still succeed in life; although much of his or her success would be due to the support and assistance of others.	
Positive Circumstances	Jia or Yi Wood penetrated to the Heavenly Stems	
Negative Circumstances	Absence of Jia Wood or Yi Wood in the Heavenly Stems.	

* Jia Wood and Geng Metal are the preferred Useful Gods for a Ding Fire Day Master born in a Chou (Ox) Month.

** The Useful Gods for a Day Master born in either a Hai (Pig), Zi (Rat) or Chou (Ox) Month are basically the same.

Day Master Ding 丁 Fire	Month Chou 丑 (Ox)

Summary

- The Useful Gods and general theories regarding a Ding Fire Day Master born in any of the winter months of Hai (Pig), Zi (Rat) or Chou (Ox) are basically the same.

- Jia Wood (Direct Resource Star) must also be accompanied by Geng Metal (Direct Wealth Star), as both are equally important as Useful Gods.

- It would be futile even attempting to substitute Jia Wood and Geng Metal with Yi Wood and Xin Metal respectively, since the latter two elements would be of no use as Useful Gods.

十二月 Twelfth Month

Ox

About Joey Yap

Joey Yap is the Founder and Master Trainer of the Mastery Academy of Chinese Metaphysics, a global organization devoted to the teaching of Feng Shui, BaZi, Mian Xiang and other Chinese Metaphysics subjects. He is also the Chief Consultant of Yap Global Consulting, an international consulting firm specialising in Feng Shui and Chinese Astrology services and audits.

He is the bestselling author of over 25 books, including *Stories and Lessons on Feng Shui, BaZi – The Destiny Code, Mian Xiang – Discover Face Reading, Feng Shui for Homebuyers Series*, and *Pure Feng Shui,* which was released by an international publisher.

He is also the producer of the first comprehensive reference source of Chinese Metaphysics, *The Chinese Metaphysics Compendium*, a compilation of all the essential formulas and applications known and practiced in Chinese Metaphysics today. He has since produced various other reference books and workbooks to aid students in their study and practice of Chinese Metaphysics subjects.

An avid proponent of technology being the way forward in disseminating knowledge of Chinese Metaphysics, Joey has developed, among others, the *BaZi Ming Pan 2.0 Software* and the *Xuan Kong Flying Stars Feng Shui Software*. This passion for fusing the best of modern technology with the best of classical studies lead him to create one of the pioneer online schools for Chinese Metaphysics education, the Mastery Academy E-Learning Centre (www.maelearning.com).

In addition to being a regular guest on various international radio and TV shows, Joey has also written columns for leading newspapers, as well as having contributed articles for various international magazines and publications. He has been featured in many popular publications and media including *Time International, Forbes International*, the *International Herald Tribune*, and Bloomberg TV, and was selected as one of Malaysia Tatler's 'Most Influential People in Malaysia' in 2008.

A naturally engaging speaker, Joey has presented to clients like Citibank, HSBC, IBM, Microsoft, Sime Darby, Bloomberg, HP, Samsung, Mah Sing, Nokia, Dijaya, and Standard Chartered.

Joey has also hosted his own TV series, *Discovering Feng Shui with Joey Yap*, and appeared on Malaysia's Astro TV network's *Walking the Dragons with Joey Yap*.

Joey's updates can be followed via Twitter at **www.twitter.com/joeyyap**. A full list of recent events and updates, and more information, can be found at **www.joeyyap.com** and **www.masteryacademy.com**

EDUCATION
The Mastery Academy of Chinese Metaphysics:
the first choice for practitioners and aspiring students of the art and science of Chinese Classical Feng Shui and Astrology.

For thousands of years, Eastern knowledge has been passed from one generation to another through the system of discipleship. A venerated master would accept suitable individuals at a young age as his disciples, and informally through the years, pass on his knowledge and skills to them. His disciples in turn, would take on their own disciples, as a means to perpetuate knowledge or skills.

This system served the purpose of restricting the transfer of knowledge to only worthy honourable individuals and ensuring that outsiders or Westerners would not have access to thousands of years of Eastern knowledge, learning and research.

However, the disciple system has also resulted in Chinese Metaphysics and Classical Studies lacking systematic teaching methods. Knowledge garnered over the years has not been accumulated in a concise, systematic manner, but scattered amongst practitioners, each practicing his/her knowledge, art and science, in isolation.

The disciple system, out of place in today's modern world, endangers the advancement of these classical fields that continue to have great relevance and application today.

At the Mastery Academy of Chinese Metaphysics, our Mission is to bring Eastern Classical knowledge in the fields of metaphysics, Feng Shui and Astrology sciences and the arts to the world. These Classical teachings and knowledge, previously shrouded in secrecy and passed on only through the discipleship system, are adapted into structured learning, which can easily be understood, learnt and mastered. Through modern learning methods, these renowned ancient arts, sciences and practices can be perpetuated while facilitating more extensive application and understanding of these classical subjects.

The Mastery Academy espouses an educational philosophy that draws from the best of the East and West. It is the world's premier educational institution for the study of Chinese Metaphysics Studies offering a wide range and variety of courses, ensuring that students have the opportunity to pursue their preferred field of study and enabling existing practitioners and professionals to gain cross-disciplinary knowledge that complements their current field of practice.

Courses at the Mastery Academy have been carefully designed to ensure a comprehensive yet compact syllabus. The modular nature of the courses enables students to immediately begin to put their knowledge into practice while pursuing continued study of their field and complementary fields. Students thus have the benefit of developing and gaining practical experience in tandem with the expansion and advancement of their theoretical knowledge.

Students can also choose from a variety of study options, from a distance learning program, the Homestudy Series, that enables study at one's own pace or intensive foundation courses and compact lecture-based courses, held in various cities around the world by Joey Yap or our licensed instructors. The Mastery Academy's faculty and make-up is international in nature, thus ensuring that prospective students can attend courses at destinations nearest to their country of origin or with a licensed Mastery Academy instructor in their home country.

The Mastery Academy provides 24x7 support to students through its Online Community, with a variety of tools, documents, forums and e-learning materials to help students stay at the forefront of research in their fields and gain invaluable assistance from peers and mentoring from their instructors.

MASTERY ACADEMY
OF CHINESE METAPHYSICS

www.masteryacademy.com

MALAYSIA
19-3, The Boulevard
Mid Valley City
59200 Kuala Lumpur, Malaysia
Tel   : +603-2284 8080
Fax   : +603-2284 1218
Email : info@masteryacademy.com

SINGAPORE
14, Robinson Road # 13-00
Far East Finance Building
Singapore 048545
Tel   : +65-6494 9147
Email : singapore@masteryacademy.com

Australia, Austria, Canada, China, Croatia, Cyprus, Czech Republic, Denmark, France, Germany, Greece, Hungary, India, Italy, Kazakhstan, Malaysia, Netherlands (Holland), New Zealand, Philippines, Poland, Russian Federation, Singapore, Slovenia, South Africa, Switzerland, Turkey, U.S.A., Ukraine, United Kingdom

Introducing...
The Mastery Academy's E-Learning Center!

The Mastery Academy's goal has always been to share authentic knowledge of Chinese Metaphysics with the whole world.

Nevertheless, we do recognize that distance, time, and hotel and traveling costs – amongst many other factors – could actually hinder people from enrolling for a classroom-based course. But with the advent and amazing advance of IT today, NOT any more!

With this in mind, we have invested heavily in IT, to conceive what is probably the first and only E-Learning Center in the world today that offers a full range of studies in the field of Chinese Metaphysics.

Convenient   Study from Your   Easy Enrollment
                     Own Home

The Mastery Academy's E-Learning Center

Now, armed with your trusty computer or laptop, and Internet access, knowledge of classical Feng Shui, BaZi (Destiny Analysis) and Mian Xiang (Face Reading) are but a literal click away!

Study at your own pace, and interact with your Instructor and fellow students worldwide, from anywhere in the world. With our E-Learning Center, knowledge of Chinese Metaphysics is brought DIRECTLY to you in all its clarity – topic-by-topic, and lesson-by-lesson; with illustrated presentations and comprehensive notes expediting your learning curve!

Your education journey through our E-Learning Center may be done via any of the following approaches:

www.maelearning.com

1. Online Courses

There are 3 Programs available: our Online Feng Shui Program, Online BaZi Program, and Online Mian Xiang Program. Each Program consists of several Levels, with each Level consisting of many Lessons in turn. Each Lesson contains a pre-recorded video session on the topic at hand, accompanied by presentation-slides and graphics as well as downloadable tutorial notes that you can print and file for future reference.

| Video Lecture | Presentation Slide | Downloadable Notes |

2. MA Live!

MA Live!, as its name implies, enables LIVE broadcasts of Joey Yap's courses and seminars – right to your computer screen. Students will not only get to see and hear Joey talk on real-time 'live', but also participate and more importantly, TALK to Joey via the MA Live! interface. All the benefits of a live class, minus the hassle of actually having to attend one!

How It Works

Our Live Classes   You at Home

3. Video-On-Demand (VOD)

Get immediate streaming-downloads of the Mastery Academy's wide range of educational DVDs, right on your computer screen. No more shipping costs and waiting time to be incurred!

Instant VOD Online

Choose From Our list of Available VODs!   Click "Play" on Your PC

Welcome to **www.maelearning.com**; the web portal of our E-Learning Center, and YOUR virtual gateway to Chinese Metaphysics!

Mastery Academy around the world

Canada

United States

Denmark

United Kingdom

Switzerland

Czech Republic
Austria

Poland

Netherlands
France   Italy
Cyprus

Germany
Slovenia   Hungary
Croatia
Greece

Russian
Federation

Ukraine

Turkey

Kazakhstan

India

China

Philippines
Kuala Lumpur
Malaysia

Singapore

Australia

New Zealand

South Africa

YAP GLOBAL CONSULTING

Joey Yap & Yap Global Consulting

Headed by Joey Yap, Yap Global Consulting (YGC) is a leading international consulting firm specializing in Feng Shui, Mian Xiang (Face Reading) and BaZi (Destiny Analysis) consulting services worldwide. Joey - an internationally renowned Master Trainer, Consultant, Speaker and best-selling Author - has dedicated his life to the art and science of Chinese Metaphysics.

YGC has its main offices in Kuala Lumpur and Australia, and draws upon its diverse reservoir of strength from a group of dedicated and experienced consultants based in more than 30 countries, worldwide.

As the pioneer in blending established, classical Chinese Metaphysics techniques with the latest approach in consultation practices, YGC has built its reputation on the principles of professionalism and only the highest standards of service. This allows us to retain the cutting edge in delivering Feng Shui and Destiny consultation services to both corporate and personal clients, in a simple and direct manner, without compromising on quality.

Across Industries: Our Portfolio of Clients

Our diverse portfolio of both corporate and individual clients from all around the world bears testimony to our experience and capabilities.

Virtually every industry imaginable has benefited from our services - ranging from academic and financial institutions, real-estate developers and multinational corporations, to those in the leisure and tourism industry. Our services are also engaged by professionals, prominent business personalities, celebrities, high-profile politicians and people from all walks of life.

YAP GLOBAL CONSULTING

ame (Mr./Mrs./Ms.):

ontact Details

el: _____ Fax: _____

Mobile : _____

-mail: _____

What Type of Consultation Are You Interested In?

☐ Feng Shui ☐ BaZi ☐ Date Selection ☐ Yi Jing

Please tick if applicable:

☐ Are you a Property Developer looking to engage Yap Global Consulting?

☐ Are you a Property Investor looking for tailor-made packages to suit your investment requirements?

Please attach your name card here.

Thank you for completing this form. Please fax it back to us at:

Singapore
Tel : +65-6494 9147

Malaysia & the rest of the world
Fax: +603-2284 2213   Tel : +603-2284 1213

Feng Shui Consultations

For Residential Properties
- Initial Land/Property Assessment
- Residential Feng Shui Consultations
- Residential Land Selection
- End-to-End Residential Consultation

For Commercial Properties
- Initial Land/Property Assessment
- Commercial Feng Shui Consultations
- Commercial Land Selection
- End-to-End Commercial Consultation

For Property Developers
- End-to-End Consultation
- Post-Consultation Advisory Services
- Panel Feng Shui Consultant

For Property Investors
- Your Personal Feng Shui Consultant
- Tailor-Made Packages

For Memorial Parks & Burial Sites
- Yin House Feng Shui

BaZi Consultations

Personal Destiny Analysis
- Personal Destiny Analysis for Individuals
- Children's BaZi Analysis
- Family BaZi Analysis

Strategic Analysis for Corporate Organizations
- Corporate BaZi Consultations
- BaZi Analysis for Human Resource Management

Entrepreneurs & Business Owners
- BaZi Analysis for Entrepreneurs

Career Pursuits
- BaZi Career Analysis

Relationships
- Marriage and Compatibility Analysis
- Partnership Analysis

For Everyone
- Annual BaZi Forecast
- Your Personal BaZi Coach**Personal Destiny Analysis**
- Personal Destiny Analysis for Individuals

Date Selection Consultations

- **Marriage Date Selection**
- **Caesarean Birth Date Selection**
- **House-Moving Date Selection**
- **Renovation & Groundbreaking Dates**

- **Signing of Contracts**
- **Official Openings**
- **Product Launches**

Yi Jing Assessment

A Time-Tested, Accurate Science

- With a history predating 4 millennia, the Yi Jing - or Classic of Change - is one of the oldest Chinese texts surviving today. Its purpose as an oracle, in predicting the outcome of things, is based on the variables of Time, Space and Specific Events.

- A Yi Jing Assessment provides specific answers to any specific questions you may have about a specific event or endeavor. This is something that a Destiny Analysis would not be able to give you.

Basically, what a Yi Jing Assessment does is focus on only ONE aspect or item at a particular point in your life, and give you a calculated prediction of the details that will follow suit, if you undertake a particular action. It gives you an insight into a situation, and what course of action to take in order to arrive at a satisfactory outcome at the end of the day.

Please Contact YGC for a personalized Yi Jing Assessment!

INVITING US TO YOUR CORPORATE EVENTS

Many reputable organizations and institutions have worked closely with YGC to build a synergistic business relationship by engaging our team of consultants, led by Joey Yap, as speakers at their corporate events. Our seminars and short talks are always packed with audiences consisting of clients and associates of multinational and public-listed companies as well as key stakeholders of financial institutions.

We tailor our seminars and talks to suit the anticipated or pertinent group of audience. Be it a department, subsidiary, your clients or even the entire corporation, we aim to fit your requirements in delivering the intended message(s).

CHINESE METAPHYSICS REFERENCE SERIES

The **Chinese Metaphysics Reference Series** is a collection of reference texts, source material, and educational textbooks to be used as supplementary guides by scholars, students, researchers, teachers and practitioners of Chinese Metaphysics.

These comprehensive and structured books provide fast, easy reference to aid in the study and practice of various Chinese Metaphysics subjects including Feng Shui, BaZi, Yi Jing, Zi Wei, Liu Ren, Ze Ri, Ta Yi, Qi Men and Mian Xiang.

The Chinese Metaphysics Compendium

At over 1,000 pages, the *Chinese Metaphysics Compendium* is a unique one-volume reference book that compiles all the formulas relating to Feng Shui, BaZi (Four Pillars of Destiny), Zi Wei (Purple Star Astrology), Yi Jing (I-Ching), Qi Men (Mystical Doorways), Ze Ri (Date Selection), Mian Xiang (Face Reading) and other sources of Chinese Metaphysics.

It is presented in the form of easy-to-read tables, diagrams and reference charts, all of which are compiled into one handy book. This first-of-its-kind compendium is presented in both English and the original Chinese, so that none of the meanings and contexts of the technical terminologies are lost.

The only essential and comprehensive reference on Chinese Metaphysics, and an absolute must-have for all students, scholars, and practitioners of Chinese Metaphysics.

Dong Gong Date Selection

Xuan Kong Da Gua Ten Thousand Year Calendar

Xuan Kong Da Gua Reference Book

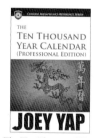

The Ten Thousand Year Calendar *(Professional Edition)*

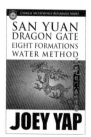

San Yuan Dragon Gate Eight Formations Water Method

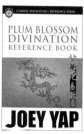

Plum Blossoms Divination Reference Book

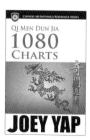

Qi Men Dun Jia 1080 Charts

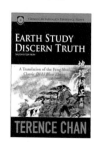

Earth Study Discern Truth Volume Two

Educational Tools & Software

Xuan Kong Flying Stars Feng Shui Software
The Essential Application for Enthusiasts and Professionals

The Xuan Kong Flying Stars Feng Shui Software is a brand-new application by Joey Yap that will assist you in the practice of Xuan Kong Feng Shui with minimum fuss and maximum effectiveness. Superimpose the Flying Stars charts over your house plans (or those of your clients) to clearly demarcate the 9 Palaces. Use it to help you create fast and sophisticated chart drawings and presentations, as well as to assist professional practitioners in the report-writing process before presenting the final reports for your clients. Students can use it to practice their Xuan Kong Feng Shui skills and knowledge, and it can even be used by designers and architects!

Some of the highlights of the software include:
- Natal Flying Stars
- Monthly Flying Stars
- 81 Flying Stars Combinations
- Dual-View Format
- Annual Flying Stars
- Flying Stars Integration
- 24 Mountains

All charts will be are printable and configurable, and can be saved for future editing. Also, you'll be able to export your charts into most image file formats like jpeg, bmp, and gif.

The Xuan Kong Flying Stars Feng Shui Software can make your Feng Shui practice simpler and more effective, garnering you amazing results with less effort!

Mini Feng Shui Compass

This Mini Feng Shui Compass with the accompanying Companion Booklet written by leading Feng Shui and Chinese Astrology Master Trainer Joey Yap is a must-have for any Feng Shui enthusiast.

The Mini Feng Shui Compass is a self-aligning compass that is not only light at 100gms but also built sturdily to ensure it will be convenient to use anywhere. The rings on the Mini Feng Shui Compass are bi-lingual and incorporate the 24 Mountain Rings that is used in your traditional Luo Pan.

The comprehensive booklet included will guide you in applying the 24 Mountain Directions on your Mini Feng Shui Compass effectively and the 8 Mansions Feng Shui to locate the most auspicious locations within your home, office and surroundings. You can also use the Mini Feng Shui Compass when measuring the direction of your property for the purpose of applying Flying Stars Feng Shui.

Educational Tools & Software

BaZi Ming Pan Software Version 2.0
Professional Four Pillars Calculator for Destiny Analysis

The BaZi Ming Pan Version 2.0 Professional Four Pillars Calculator for Destiny Analysis is the most technically advanced software of its kind in the world today. It allows even those without any knowledge of BaZi to generate their own BaZi Charts, and provides virtually every detail required to undertake a comprehensive Destiny Analysis.

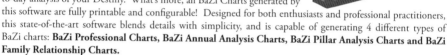

This Professional Four Pillars Calculator allows you to even undertake a day-to-day analysis of your Destiny. What's more, all BaZi Charts generated by this software are fully printable and configurable! Designed for both enthusiasts and professional practitioners, this state-of-the-art software blends details with simplicity, and is capable of generating 4 different types of BaZi charts: **BaZi Professional Charts, BaZi Annual Analysis Charts, BaZi Pillar Analysis Charts and BaZi Family Relationship Charts.**

Additional references, configurable to cater to all levels of BaZi knowledge and usage, include:
• Dual Age & Bilingual Option (Western & Chinese) • Na Yin narrations • 12 Life Stages evaluation • Death & Emptiness • Gods & Killings • Special Days • Heavenly Virtue Nobles

This software also comes with a Client Management feature that allows you to save and trace clients' records instantly, navigate effortlessly between BaZi charts, and file your clients' information in an organized manner.

The BaZi Ming Pan Version 2.0 Calculator sets a new standard by combining the best of BaZi and technology.

Joey Yap Feng Shui Template Set

Directions are the cornerstone of any successful Feng Shui audit or application. The **Joey Yap Feng Shui Template Set** is a set of three templates to simplify the process of taking directions and determining locations and positions, whether it's for a building, a house, or an open area such as a plot of land, all with just a floor plan or area map.

The Set comprises 3 basic templates: The Basic Feng Shui Template, 8 Mansions Feng Shui Template, and the Flying Stars Feng Shui Template.

With bi-lingual notations for these directions; both in English and the original Chinese, the **Joey Yap Feng Shui Template Set** comes with its own Booklet that gives simple yet detailed instructions on how to make use of the 3 templates within.

• Easy-to-use, simple, and straightforward
• Small and portable; each template measuring only 5" x 5"
• Additional 8 Mansions and Flying Stars Reference Rings
• Handy companion booklet with usage tips and examples

Accelerate Your Face Reading Skills With Joey Yap's Face Reading Revealed DVD Series

Mian Xiang, the Chinese art of Face Reading, is an ancient form of physiognomy and entails the use of the face and facial characteristics to evaluate key aspects of a person's life, luck and destiny. In his Face Reading DVDs series, Joey Yap shows you how the facial features reveal a wealth of information about a person's luck, destiny and personality.

Mian Xiang also tell us the talents, quirks and personality of an individual. Do you know that just by looking at a person's face, you can ascertain his or her health, wealth, relationships and career? Let Joey Yap show you how the 12 Palaces can be utilised to reveal a person's inner talents, characteristics and much more.

Each facial feature on the face represents one year in a person's life. Your face is a 100-year map of your life and each position reveals your fortune and destiny at a particular age as well as insights and information about your personality, skills, abilities and destiny.

Using Mian Xiang, you will also be able to plan your life ahead by identifying, for example, the right business partner and knowing the sort of person that you need to avoid. By knowing their characteristics through the facial features, you will be able to gauge their intentions and gain an upper hand in negotiations.

Do you know what moles signify? Do they bring good or bad luck? Do you want to build better relationships with your partner or family members or have your ever wondered why you seem to be always bogged down by trivial problems in your life?

In these highly entertaining DVDs, Joey will help you answer all these questions and more. You will be able to ascertain the underlying meaning of moles, birthmarks or even the type of your hair in Face Reading. Joey will also reveal the guidelines to help you foster better and stronger relationships with your loved ones through Mian Xiang.

Feng Shui for Homebuyers DVD Series

Best-selling Author, and international Master Trainer and Consultant Joey Yap reveals in these DVDs the significant Feng Shui features that every homebuyer should know when evaluating a property.

Joey will guide you on how to customise your home to maximise the Feng Shui potential of your property and gain the full benefit of improving your health, wealth and love life using the 9 Palace Grid. He will show you how to go about applying the classical applications of the Life Gua and House Gua techniques to get attuned to your Sheng Qi (positive energies).

In these DVDs, you will also learn how to identify properties with good Feng Shui features that will help you promote a fulfilling life and achieve your full potential. Discover how to avoid properties with negative Feng Shui that can bring about detrimental effects to your health, wealth and relationships.

Joey will also elaborate on how to fix the various aspects of your home that may have an impact on the Feng Shui of your property and give pointers on how to tap into the positive energies to support your goals.

Discover Feng Shui with Joey Yap (TV Series)

Discover Feng Shui with Joey Yap: Set of 4 DVDs

Informative and entertaining, classical Feng Shui comes alive in *Discover Feng Shui with Joey Yap!*

Dying to know how you can use Feng Shui to improve your house or office, but simply too busy attend for formal classes?

You have the questions. Now let Joey personally answer them in this 4-set DVD compilation! Learn how to ensure the viability of your residence or workplace, Feng Shui-wise, without having to convert it into a Chinese antiques' shop. Classical Feng Shui is about harnessing the natural power of your environment to improve quality of life. It's a systematic and subtle metaphysical science.

And that's not all. Joey also debunks many a myth about classical Feng Shui, and shares with viewers Face Reading tips as well!

Own the series that national channel 8TV did a re-run of in 2005, today!

Annual Releases

Chinese Astrology for 2009

This information-packed annual guide to the Chinese Astrology for 2009 goes way beyond the conventional 'animal horoscope' book. To begin with, author Joey Yap includes a personalized outlook for 2009 based on the individual's BaZi Day Pillar (Jia Zi) and a 12-month micro-analysis for each of the 60 Day Pillars – in addition to the annual outlook for all 12 animal signs and the 12-month outlook for each animal sign in 2009. Find out what awaits you in 2009 from the four key aspects of Health, Wealth, Career and Relationships…with Joey Yap's **Chinese Astrology for 2009**!

Feng Shui for 2009

Maximize the Qi of the Year of the Earth Rat for your home and office, with Joey Yap's **Feng Shui for 2009** book. Learn how to tap into the positive sectors of the year, and avoid the negative ones and those with the Annual Afflictions, as well as ascertain how the annual Flying Stars affect your property by comparing them against the Eight Mansions (Ba Zhai) for 2009. Flying Stars enthusiasts will also find this book handy, as it includes the monthly Flying Stars charts for the year, accompanied by detailed commentaries on what sectors to use and avoid – to enable you to optimize your Academic, Relationships and Wealth Luck in 2009.

Tong Shu Diary 2009

Organize your professional and personal lives with the **Tong Shu Diary 2009**, with a twist… it also allows you to determine the most suitable dates on which you can undertake important activities and endeavors throughout the year! This compact Diary integrates the Chinese Solar and Lunar Calendars with the universal lingua franca of the Gregorian Calendar.

Tong Shu Monthly Planner 2009

Tailor-made for the Feng Shui or BaZi enthusiast in you, or even professional Chinese Metaphysics consultants who want a compact planner with useful information incorporated into it. In the **Tong Shu Monthly Planner 2009**, you will find the auspicious and inauspicious dates for the year marked out for you, alongside the most suitable activities to be undertaken on each day. As a bonus, there is also a reference section containing all the monthly Flying Stars charts and Annual Afflictions for 2009.

Tong Shu Desktop Calendar 2009

Get an instant snapshot of the suitable and unsuitable activities for each day of the Year of the Earth Rat, with the icons displayed on this lightweight Desktop Calendar. Elegantly presenting the details of the Chinese Solar Calendar in the form of the standard Gregorian one, the **Tong Shu Desktop Calendar 2009** is perfect for Chinese Metaphysics enthusiasts and practitioners alike. Whether it a business launching or meeting, ground breaking ceremony, travel or house-moving that you have in mind, this Calendar is designed to fulfill your information needs.

Tong Shu Year Planner 2009

This one-piece Planner presents you all the essential information you need for significant activities or endeavors…with just a quick glance! In a nutshell, it allows you to identify the favorable and unfavorable days, which will in turn enable you to schedule your year's activities so as to make the most of good days, and avoid the ill-effects brought about by inauspicious ones.

Continue Your Journey with Joey Yap's Books

Walking the Dragons

Walking the Dragons is a guided tour through the classical landform Feng Shui of ancient China, an enchanting collection of deeply-researched yet entertaining essays rich in historical detail.

Compiled in one book for the first time from Joey Yap's Feng Shui Mastery Excursion Series, the book highlights China's extensive, vibrant history with astute observations on the Feng Shui of important sites and places. Learn the landform formations of Yin Houses (tombs and burial places), as well as mountains, temples, castles, and villages.

It demonstrates complex Feng Shui theories and principles in easy-to-understand, entertaining language and is the perfect addition to the bookshelf of a Feng Shui or history lover. Anyone, whether experienced in Feng Shui or new to the practice, will be able to enjoy the insights shared in this book. Complete with gorgeous full-colour pictures of all the amazing sights and scenery, it's the next best thing to having been there yourself!

Your Aquarium Here

Your Aquarium Here is a simple, practical, hands-on Feng Shui book that teaches you how to incorporate a Water feature – an aquarium – for optimal Feng Shui benefit, whether for personal relationships, wealth, or career. Designed to be comprehensive yet simple enough for a novice or beginner, *Your Aquarium Here* provides historical and factual information about the role of Water in Feng Shui, and provides a step-by-step guide to installing and using an aquarium.

The book is the first in the **Fengshuilogy Series**, a series of matter-of-fact and useful Feng Shui books designed for the person who wants to do fuss-free Feng Shui. Not everyone who wants to use Feng Shui is an expert or a scholar! This series of books are just the kind you'd want on your bookshelf to gain basic, practical knowledge of the subject. Go ahead and Feng Shui-It-Yourself – *Your Aquarium Here* eliminates all the fuss and bother, but maintains all the fun and excitement, of authentic Feng Shui application!

The Art of Date Selection: Personal Date Selection

In today's modern world, it is not good enough to just do things effectively – we need to do them efficiently, as well. From the signing of business contracts and moving into a new home, to launching a product or even tying the knot; everything has to move, and move very quickly too. There is a premium on Time, where mistakes can indeed be costly.

The notion of doing the Right Thing, at the Right Time and in the Right Place is the very backbone of Date Selection. Because by selecting a suitable date specially tailored to a specific activity or endeavor, we infuse it with the most positive energies prevalent in our environment during that particular point in time; and that could well make the difference between 'make-and-break'! With the *Art of Date Selection: Personal Date Selection*, learn simple, practical methods you can employ to select not just good dates, but personalized good dates. Whether it's a personal activity such as a marriage or professional endeavor such as launching a business, signing a contract or even acquiring assets, this book will show you how to pick the good dates and tailor them to suit the activity in question, as well as avoid the negative ones too!

The Art of Date Selection: Feng Shui Date Selection

Date Selection is the Art of selecting the most suitable date, where the energies present on the day support the specific activities or endeavors we choose to undertake on that day. Feng Shui is the Chinese Metaphysical study of the Physiognomy of the Land – landforms and the Qi they produce, circulate and conduct. Hence, anything that exists on this Earth is invariably subject to the laws of Feng Shui. So what do we get when Date Selection and Feng Shui converge?

Feng Shui Date Selection, of course! Say you wish to renovate your home, or maybe buy or rent one. Or perhaps, you're a developer, and wish to know WHEN is the best date possible to commence construction works on your project. In any case – and all cases – you certainly wish to ensure that your endeavors are well supported by the positive energies present on a good day, won't you? And this is where Date Selection supplements the practice of Feng Shui. At the end of the day, it's all about making the most of what's good, and minimizing what's bad.

(Available Soon)

Continue Your Journey with Joey Yap's Books

Feng Shui For Homebuyers - Exterior

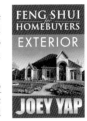

Best selling Author and international Feng Shui Consultant, Joey Yap, will guide you on the various important features in your external environment that have a bearing on the Feng Shui of your home. For homeowners, those looking to build their own home or even investors who are looking to apply Feng Shui to their homes, this book provides valuable information from the classical Feng Shui theories and applications.

This book will assist you in screening and eliminating unsuitable options with negative FSQ (Feng Shui Quotient) should you acquire your own land or if you are purchasing a newly built home. It will also help you in determining which plot of land to select and which to avoid when purchasing an empty parcel of land.

Feng Shui for Homebuyers - Interior

A book every homeowner or potential house buyer should have. The Feng Shui for Homebuyers (Interior) is an informative reference book and invaluable guide written by best selling Author and international Feng Shui Consultant, Joey Yap.

This book provides answers to the important questions of what really does matter when looking at the internal Feng Shui of a home or office. It teaches you how to analyze your home or office floor plans and how to improve their Feng Shui. It will answer all your questions about the positive and negative flow of Qi within your home and ways to utilize them to your maximum benefit.

Providing you with a guide to calculating your Life Gua and House Gua to fine-tune your Feng Shui within your property, Joey Yap focuses on practical, easily applicable ideas on what you can implement internally in a property.

Feng Shui for Apartment Buyers - Home Owners

Finding a good apartment or condominium is never an easy task but who do you ensure that is also has good Feng Shui? And how exactly do you apply Feng Shui to an apartment or condominium or high-rise residence?

These questions and more are answered by renowned Feng Shui Consultant and Master Trainer Joey Yap in **Feng Shui for Apartment Buyers - Home Owners**. Joey answers the key questions about Feng Shui and apartments, then guides you through the bare basics like taking a direction and super-imposing a Flying Stars chart onto a floor plan. Joey also walks you through the process of finding an apartment with favorable Feng Shui, sharing with you some of the key methods and techniques that are employed by professional Feng Shui consultants in assesing apartment Feng Shui.

In his trademark straight-to-the-point manner, Joey shares with you the Feng Shui do's and dont's when it comes to finding an apartment with favorable Feng Shui and which is conducive for home living.

The Ten Thousand Year Calendar

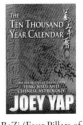

The Ten Thousand Year Calendar or 萬年曆 Wan Nian Li is a regular reference book and an invaluable tool used by masters, practitioners and students of Feng Shui, BaZi (Four Pillars of Destiny), Chinese Zi Wei Dou Shu Astrology (Purple Star), Yi Jing (I-Ching) and Date Selection specialists.

JOEY YAP's *Ten Thousand Year Calendar* provides the Gregorian (Western) dates converted into both the Chinese Solar and Lunar calendar in both the English and Chinese language.

It also includes a comprehensive set of key Feng Shui and Chinese Astrology charts and references, including Xuan Kong Nine Palace Flying Star Charts, Monthly and Daily Flying Stars, Water Dragon Formulas Reference Charts, Zi Wei Dou Shu (Purple Star) Astrology Reference Charts, BaZi (Four Pillars of Destiny) Heavenly Stems, Earthly Branches and all other related reference tables for Chinese Metaphysical Studies.

Continue Your Journey with Joey Yap's Books

Stories and Lessons on Feng Shui (English & Chinese versions)

Stories and Lessons on Feng Shui is a compilation of essays and stories written by leading Feng Shui and Chinese Astrology trainer and consultant Joey Yap about Feng Shui and Chinese Astrology.

In this heart-warming collection of easy to read stories, find out why it's a myth that you should never have Water on the right hand side of your house, the truth behind the infamous 'love' and 'wealth' corners and that the sudden death of a pet fish is really NOT due to bad luck!

More Stories and Lessons on Feng Shui

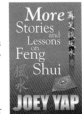

Finally, the long-awaited sequel to *Stories & Lessons on Feng Shui*!

If you've read the best-selling Stories & Lessons on Feng Shui, you won't want to miss this book. And even if you haven't read *Stories & Lessons on Feng Shui*, there's always a time to rev your Feng Shui engine up.

The time is NOW.

And the book? *More Stories & Lessons on Feng Shui* – the 2nd compilation of the most popular articles and columns penned by Joey Yap; **specially featured in national and international publications, magazines and newspapers.**

All in all, *More Stories & Lessons on Feng Shui* is a delightful chronicle of Joey's articles, thoughts and vast experience - as a professional Feng Shui consultant and instructor - that have been purposely refined, edited and expanded upon to make for a light-hearted, interesting yet educational read. And with Feng Shui, BaZi, Mian Xiang and Yi Jing all thrown into this one dish, there's something for everyone…so all you need to serve or accompany *More Stories & Lessons on Feng Shui* with is your favorite cup of tea or coffee!

Even More Stories and Lessons on Feng Shui

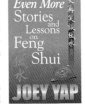

In this third release in the Stories and Lessons series, Joey Yap continues his exploration on the study and practice of Feng Shui in the modern age through a series of essays and personal anecdotes. Debunking superstition, offering simple and understandable "Feng Shui-It-Yourself" tips, and expounding on the history and origins of classical Feng Shui, Joey takes readers on a journey that is always refreshing and exciting.

Besides 'behind-the-scenes' revelations of actual Feng Shui audits, there are also chapters on how beginners can easily and accurately incorporate Feng Shui practice into their lives, as well as travel articles that offer proof that when it comes to Feng Shui, the Qi literally knows no boundaries.

In his trademark lucid and forthright style, Joey covers themes and topics that will strike a chord with all readers who have an interest in Feng Shui.

Mian Xiang - Discover Face Reading

Need to identify a suitable business partner? How about understanding your staff or superiors better? Or even choosing a suitable spouse? These mind boggling questions can be answered in Joey Yap's introductory book to Face Reading titled *Mian Xiang – Discover Face Reading*. This book will help you discover the hidden secrets in a person's face.

Mian Xiang – Discover Face Reading is comprehensive book on all areas of Face Reading, covering some of the most important facial features, including the forehead, mouth, ears and even the philtrum above your lips. This book will help you analyse not just your Destiny but help you achieve your full potential and achieve life fulfillment.

Continue Your Journey with Joey Yap's Books

BaZi - The Destiny Code (English & Chinese versions)

Leading Chinese Astrology Master Trainer Joey Yap makes it easy to learn how to unlock your Destiny through your BaZi with this book. BaZi or Four Pillars of Destiny is an ancient Chinese science which enables individuals to understand their personality, hidden talents and abilities as well as their luck cycle, simply by examining the information contained within their birth data. The Destiny Code is the first book that shows readers how to plot and interpret their own Destiny Charts and lays the foundation for more in-depth BaZi studies. Written in a lively entertaining style, the Destiny Code makes BaZi accessible to the layperson. Within 10 chapters, understand and appreciate more about this astoundingly accurate ancient Chinese Metaphysical science.

BaZi - The Destiny Code Revealed

In this follow up to Joey Yap's best-selling The Destiny Code, delve deeper into your own Destiny chart through an understanding of the key elemental relationships that affect the Heavenly Stems and Earthly Branches. Find out how Combinations, Clash, Harm, Destructions and Punishments bring new dimension to a BaZi chart. Complemented by extensive real-life examples, The Destiny Code Revealed takes you to the next level of BaZi, showing you how to unlock the Codes of Destiny and to take decisive action at the right time, and capitalise on the opportunities in life.

Xuan Kong: Flying Stars Feng Shui

Xuan Kong Flying Stars Feng Shui is an essential introductory book to the subject of Xuan Kong Fei Xing, a well-known and popular system of Feng Shui, written by International Feng Shui Master Trainer Joey Yap.

In his down-to-earth, entertaining and easy to read style, Joey Yap takes you through the essential basics of Classical Feng Shui, and the key concepts of Xuan Kong Fei Xing (Flying Stars). Learn how to fly the stars, plot a Flying Star chart for your home or office and interpret the stars and star combinations. Find out how to utilise the favourable areas of your home or office for maximum benefit and learn 'tricks of the trade' and 'trade secrets' used by Feng Shui practitioners to enhance and maximise Qi in your home or office.

An essential integral introduction to the subject of Classical Feng Shui and the Flying Stars System of Feng Shui!

Xuan Kong Flying Stars: Structures and Combinations

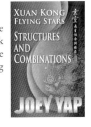

Delve deeper into Flying Stars through a greater understanding of the 81 Combinations and the influence of the Annual and Monthly Stars on the Base, Sitting and Facing Stars in this 2nd book in the Xuan Kong Feng Shui series. Learn how Structures like the Combination of 10, Up the Mountain and Down the River, Pearl and Parent String Structures are used to interpret a Flying Star chart.

(Available Soon)

Xuan Kong Flying Stars: Advanced Techniques

Take your knowledge of Xuan Kong Flying Stars to a higher level and learn how to apply complex techniques and advanced formulas such as Castle Gate Technique, Seven Star Robbery Formation, Advancing the Dragon Formation and Replacement Star technique amongst others. Joey Yap also shows you how to use the Life Palace technique to combine Gua Numbers with Flying Star numbers and utilise the predictive facets of Flying Stars Feng Shui.

(Available Soon)

Elevate Your Feng Shui Skills With Joey Yap's Home Study Course And Educational DVDs

Xuan Kong Vol.1
An Advanced Feng Shui Home Study Course

Learn the Xuan Kong Flying Star Feng Shui system in just 20 lessons! Joey Yap's specialised notes and course work have been written to enable distance learning without compromising on the breadth or quality of the syllabus. Learn at your own pace with the same material students in a live class would use. The most comprehensive distance learning course on Xuan Kong Flying Star Feng Shui in the market. Xuan Kong Flying Star Vol.1 comes complete with a special binder for all your course notes.

Feng Shui for Period 8 - (DVD)

Don't miss the Feng Shui Event of the next 20 years! Catch Joey Yap LIVE and find out just what Period 8 is all about. This DVD boxed set zips you through the fundamentals of Feng Shui and the impact of this important change in the Feng Shui calendar. Joey's entertaining, conversational style walks you through the key changes that Period 8 will bring and how to tap into Wealth Qi and Good Feng Shui for the next 20 years.

Xuan Kong Flying Stars Beginners Workshop - (DVD)

Take a front row seat in Joey Yap's Xuan Kong Flying Stars workshop with this unique LIVE RECORDING of Joey Yap's Xuan Kong Flying Stars Feng Shui workshop, attended by over 500 people. This DVD program provides an effective and quick introduction of Xuan Kong Feng Shui essentials for those who are just starting out in their study of classical Feng Shui. Learn to plot your own Flying Star chart in just 3 hours. Learn 'trade secret' methods, remedies and cures for Flying Stars Feng Shui. This boxed set contains 3 DVDs and 1 workbook with notes and charts for reference.

BaZi Four Pillars of Destiny Beginners Workshop - (DVD)

Ever wondered what Destiny has in store for you? Or curious to know how you can learn more about your personality and inner talents? BaZi or Four Pillars of Destiny is an ancient Chinese science that enables us to understand a person's hidden talent, inner potential, personality, health and wealth luck from just their birth data. This specially compiled DVD set of Joey Yap's BaZi Beginners Workshop provides a thorough and comprehensive introduction to BaZi. Learn how to read your own chart and understand your own luck cycle. This boxed set contains 3 DVDs and 1 workbook with notes and reference charts.

Interested in learning MORE about Feng Shui? Advance Your Feng Shui Knowledge with the Mastery Academy Courses.

Feng Shui Mastery Series™
LIVE COURSES (MODULES ONE TO FOUR)

Feng Shui Mastery – Module One
Beginners Course

Designed for students seeking an entry-level intensive program into the study of Feng Shui , Module One is an intensive foundation course that aims not only to provide you with an introduction to Feng Shui theories and formulas and equip you with the skills and judgments to begin practicing and conduct simple Feng Shui audits upon successful completion of the course. Learn all about Forms, Eight Mansions Feng Shui and Flying Star Feng Shui in just one day with a unique, structured learning program that makes learning Feng Shui quick and easy!

Feng Shui Mastery – Module Two
Practitioners Course

Building on the knowledge and foundation in classical Feng Shui theory garnered in M1, M2 provides a more advanced and in-depth understanding of Eight Mansions, Xuan Kong Flying Star and San He and introduces students to theories that are found only in the classical Chinese Feng Shui texts. This 3-Day Intensive course hones analytical and judgment skills, refines Luo Pan (Chinese Feng Shui compass) skills and reveals 'trade secret' remedies. Module Two covers advanced Forms Analysis, San He's Five Ghost Carry Treasure formula, Advanced Eight Mansions and Xuan Kong Flying Stars and equips you with the skills needed to undertake audits and consultations for residences and offices.

Feng Shui Mastery – Module Three
Advanced Practitioners Course

Module Three is designed for Professional Feng Shui Practitioners. Learn advanced topics in Feng Shui and take your skills to a cutting edge level. Be equipped with the knowledge, techniques and confidence to conduct large scale audits (like estate and resort planning). Learn how to apply different systems appropriately to remedy situations or cases deemed inauspicious by one system and reconcile conflicts in different systems of Feng Shui. Gain advanced knowledge of San He (Three Harmony) systems and San Yuan (Three Cycles) systems, advanced Luan Tou (Forms Feng Shui) and specialist Water Formulas.

Feng Shui Mastery – Module Four
Master Course

The graduating course of the Feng Shui Mastery (FSM) Series, this course takes th advanced practitioner to the Master level. Power packed M4 trains students to 'wa the mountains' and identify superior landform, superior grade structures and ma qualitative evaluations of landform, structures, Water and Qi and covers advanced ¿ exclusive topics of San He, San Yuan, Xuan Kong, Ba Zhai, Luan Tou (Advanced Fo and Water Formula) Feng Shui. Master Internal, External and Luan Tou (Landfc Feng Shui methodologies to apply Feng Shui at every level and undertake consulta of every scale and magnitude, from houses and apartments to housing estates, town shopping malls and commercial districts.

BaZi Mastery Series™
LIVE COURSES (MODULES ONE TO FOUR)

BaZi Mastery – Module One
Intensive Foundation Course

This Intensive One Day Foundation Course provides an introduction to the principles and fundamentals of BaZi (Four Pillars of Destiny) and Destiny Analysis methods such as Ten Gods, Useful God and Strength of Qi. Learn how to plot a BaZi chart and interpret your Destiny and your potential. Master BaZi and learn to capitalize on your strengths, minimize risks and downturns and take charge of your Destiny.

BaZi Mastery – Module Two
Practical BaZi Applications

BaZi Module Two teaches students advanced BaZi analysis techniques and specific analysis methods for relationship luck, health evaluation, wealth potential and career potential. Students will learn to identify BaZi chart structures, sophisticated methods for applying the Ten Gods, and how to read Auxiliary Stars. Students who have completed Module Two will be able to conduct professional BaZi readings.

BaZi Mastery – Module Three
Advanced Practitioners Program

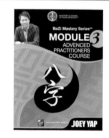

Designed for the BaZi practitioner, learn how to read complex cases and unique events in BaZi charts and perform Big and Small assessments. Discover how to analyze personalities and evaluate talents precisely, as well as special formulas and classical methodologies for BaZi from classics such as Di Tian Sui and Qiong Tong Bao Jian.

BaZi Mastery – Module Four
Master Course in BaZi

The graduating course of the BaZi Mastery Series, this course takes the advanced practitioner to the Masters' level. BaZi M4 focuses on specialized techniques of BaZi reading, unique special structures and advance methods from ancient classical texts. This program includes techniques on date selection and ancient methodologies from the Qiong Tong Bao Jian and Yuan Hai Zi Ping classics.

XUAN KONG MASTERY SERIES™
LIVE COURSES (MODULES ONE TO THREE)
* Advanced Courses For Master Practitioners

Xuan Kong Mastery – Module One
Advanced Foundation Program

This course is for the experienced Feng Shui professionals who wish to expand their knowledge and skills in the Xuan Kong system of Feng Shui, covering important foundation methods and techniques from the Wu Chang and Guang Dong lineages of Xuan Kong Feng Shui.

Xuan Kong Mastery – Module Two A
Advanced Xuan Kong Methodologies

Designed for Feng Shui practitioners seeking to specialise in the Xuan Kong system, this program focuses on methods of application and Joey Yap's unique Life Palace and Shifting Palace Methods, as well as methods and techniques from the Wu Chang lineage.

Xuan Kong Mastery – Module Two B
Purple White

Explore in detail and in great depth the star combinations in Xuan Kong. Learn how each different combination reacts or responds in different palaces, under different environmental circumstances and to whom in the property. Learn methods, theories and techniques extracted from ancient classics such as Xuan Kong Mi Zhi, Xuan Kong Fu, Fei Xing Fu and Zi Bai Jue.

Xuan Kong Mastery – Module Three
Advanced Xuan Kong Da Gua

This intensive course focuses solely on the Xuan Kong Da Gua system covering the theories, techniques and methods of application of this unique 64-Hexagram based system of Xuan Kong including Xuan Kong Da Gua for landform analysis.

Walk the Mountains! Learn Feng Shui in a Practical and Hands-on Program

Feng Shui Mastery Excursion Series™ : CHINA

Learn landform (Luan Tou) Feng Shui by walking the mountains and chasing the Dragon's vein in China. This Program takes the students in a study tour to examine notable Feng Shui landmarks, mountains, hills, valleys, ancient palaces, famous mansions, houses and tombs in China. The Excursion is a 'practical' hands-on course where students are shown to perform readings using the formulas they've learnt and to recognize and read Feng Shui Landform (Luan Tou) formations.

Read about China Excursion here:
http://www.masteryacademy.com/Education/schoolfengshui/fengshuimasteryexcursion.asp

Mian Xiang Mastery Series™
LIVE COURSES (MODULES ONE AND TWO)

Mian Xiang Mastery – Module One
Basic Face Reading

A person's face is their fortune – learn more about the ancient Chinese art of Face Reading. In just one day, be equipped with techniques and skills to read a person's face and ascertain their character, luck, wealth and relationship luck.

Mian Xiang Mastery – Module Two
Practical Face Reading

Mian Xiang Module Two covers face reading techniques extracted from the ancient classics Shen Xiang Quan Pian and Shen Xiang Tie Guan Dau. Gain a greater depth and understanding of Mian Xiang and learn to recognize key structures and characteristics in a person's face.

Yi Jing Mastery Series™
LIVE COURSES (MODULES ONE AND TWO)

Yi Jing Mastery – Module One
Traditional Yi Jing

'Yi', relates to change. Change is the only constant in life and the universe, without exception to this rule. The Yi Jing is hence popularly referred to as the Book or Classic of Change. Discoursed in the language of Yin and Yang, the Yi Jing is one of the oldest Chinese classical texts surviving today. With Traditional Yi Jing, learnn how this Classic is used to divine the outcomes of virtually every facet of life; from your relationships to seeking an answer to the issues you may face in your daily life.

Yi Jing Mastery – Module Two
Plum Blossom Numerology

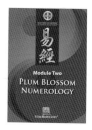

Shao Yong, widely regarded as one of the greatest scholars of the Sung Dynasty, developed Mei Hua Yi Shu (Plum Blossom Numerology) as a more advanced means for divination purpose using the Yi Jing. In Plum Blossom Numerology, the results of a hexagram are interpreted by referring to the Gua meanings, where the interaction and relationship between the five elements, stems, branches and time are equally taken into consideration. This divination method, properly applied, allows us to make proper decisions whenever we find ourselves in a predicament.

Ze Ri Mastery Series™
LIVE COURSES (MODULES ONE AND TWO)

Ze Ri Mastery Series Module 1
Personal and Feng Shui Date Selection

The Mastery Academy's Date Selection Mastery Series Module 1 is specifically structured to provide novice students with an exciting introduction to the Art of Date Selection. Learn the rudiments and tenets of this intriguing metaphysical science. What makes a good date, and what makes a bad date? What dates are suitable for which activities, and what dates simply aren't? And of course, the mother of all questions: WHY aren't all dates created equal. All in only one Module – Module 1!

Ze Ri Mastery Series Module 2
Xuan Kong Da Gua Date Selection

In Module 2, discover advanced Date Selection techniques that will take your knowledge of this Art to a level equivalent to that of a professional's! This is the Module where Date Selection infuses knowledge of the ancient metaphysical science of Feng Shui and BaZi (Chinese Astrology, or Four Pillars of Destiny). Feng Shui, as a means of maximizing Human Luck (i.e. our luck on Earth), is often quoted as the cure to BaZi, which allows us to decipher our Heaven (i.e. inherent) Luck. And one of the most potent ways of making the most of what life has to offer us is to understand our Destiny, know how we can use the natural energies of our environment for our environments and MOST importantly, WHEN we should use these energies and for WHAT endeavors!

You will learn specific methods on how to select suitable dates, tailored to specific activities and events. More importantly, you will also be taught how to suit dates to a person's BaZi (Chinese Astrology, or Four Pillars of Destiny), in order to maximize his or her strengths, and allow this person to surmount any challenges that lie in wait. Add in the factor of `place', and you would have satisfied the notion of `doing the right thing, at the right time and in the right place'! A basic knowledge of BaZi and Feng Shui will come in handy in this Module, although these are not pre-requisites to successfully undergo Module 2.

Feng Shui for Life

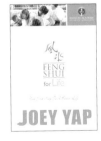

Feng Shui for life is a 5-day course designed for the Feng Shui beginner to learn how to apply practical Feng Shui in day-to-day living. It is a culmination of powerful tools and techniques that allows you to gain quick proficiency in Classical Feng Shui. Discover quick tips on analysing your own BaZi, how to apply Feng Shui solutions for your own home, how to select auspicious dates for important activities, as well as simple and useful Face Reading techniques and practical Water Formulas. This is a complete beginner's course that is suitable for anyone with an interest in applying practical, real-world Feng Shui for life! Enhance every aspect of your life – your health, wealth, and relationships – using these easy-to-apply Classical Feng Shui methods.